D0756565

TITANIC

TITANIC

THE REAL STORY OF THE CONSTRUCTION
OF THE WORLD'S MOST FAMOUS SHIP

Anton Gill

Books

TRANSWORLD PUBLISHERS
61–63 Uxbridge Road, London W5 5SA
A Random House Group Company
www.transworldbooks.co.uk

**TITANIC: THE REAL STORY OF THE CONSTRUCTION
OF THE WORLD'S MOST FAMOUS SHIP
A CHANNEL 4 BOOK: 9781905026746**

First published in Great Britain
in 2010 by Channel 4 Books
an imprint of Transworld Publishers
Channel 4 Books paperback edition published 2012

Text copyright © Anton Gill 2010, 2012

Anton Gill has asserted his right under the Copyright, Designs
and Patents Act 1988 to be identified as the author of this work.

Addresses for Random House Group Ltd companies outside the UK
can be found at: www.randomhouse.co.uk
The Random House Group Ltd Reg. No. 954009

The Random House Group Limited supports the Forest Stewardship Council
(FSC®), the leading international forest-certification organization. Our books
carrying the FSC label are printed on FSC®-certified paper. FSC is the only
forest-certification scheme endorsed by the leading environmental organizations,
including Greenpeace. Our paper procurement policy can be found at
www.randomhouse.co.uk/environment.

Typeset in11.5/15.5pt Fairfield Light by Falcon Oast Graphic Art Ltd.
Printed and bound by CPI Group (UK) Ltd, Croydon, CR0 4YY.

2 4 6 8 10 9 7 5 3 1

MIX
Paper from
responsible sources
FSC® C016897

'When anyone asks me how I can best describe my experience in nearly forty years at sea, I merely say, uneventful. Of course there have been winter gales, and storms and fog and the like. But in all my experience, I have never been in any accident of any sort worth speaking about. I have seen but one vessel in distress in all my years at sea. I never saw a wreck and never have been wrecked nor was I ever in any predicament that threatened to end in disaster of any sort.'

EDWARD J. SMITH, RD, RNR, CAPTAIN OF THE
TITANIC, HIS LAST COMMAND BEFORE RETIREMENT

CONTENTS

ACKNOWLEDGEMENTS

N O WORK OF NON-FICTION can be written without the advice, help and input of a great many people, and this work is no exception. I have particularly to thank the following individuals: Julian Alexander of LAW, my literary agent; Jonathan Barker, MBE, for advice on contemporary poetry; Bruce Beveridge, principal author of the masterly two-volume study *Titanic: The Ship Magnificent*, for clarification of certain technical points; my wife, Marji Campi, descended from four generations of Liverpudlian seafarers, for reading the manuscript with her usual hawk-eyed attention; my stepson Matthew Campi; Stuart Ellis; Sir John Hammerton; Rebecca Jones and Doug Young of Transworld Publishers; Brian Robinson for sharing his Belfast grandfather's memories with me; and Carlton Wallace. I also wish to thank Spencer Kelly, the Series Producer; Sam Whittaker, the Executive Producer; and all the production team, crew, consultants and staff at Twenty Twenty Television, creators of the documentary series that this book accompanies. Thanks also should go to Hadrian Spooner and his colleagues from HMS Engineering, who I met on location, and of course to the vast number of other contributors who took part in the series. Special thanks should go to the cast of engineers who participated in the project, Yewande Akinola, Luke Perry, Brendan Walker and Dave Wilkes, who put up with me as I wandered around asking questions while they were filming and working on their projects.

I also acknowledge with thanks the help of the following businesses, institutions and organizations: the British Library; Harland & Wolff; John Sandoe's Bookshop; the National Archives of Ireland; the National Archives, Kew; the National Maritime Museum; the Public Record Office of Northern Ireland; and the Ulster Folk and Transport Museum.

Last but not least I acknowledge the authors of the works listed in the bibliography. Their excellent and exhaustive books should be regarded as a must for any reader who, having read the present volume, wishes to expand and deepen her or his knowledge of *Titanic* and other great passenger liners.

Any work of non-fiction, however carefully checked, may be liable to contain some errors, and *Titanic*'s story, though well documented, contains many disputed elements and several lacunae. In terms of the disaster that befell the ship, there is still controversy concerning cover-ups in the subsequent inquiries, the matter of the decision to reduce the number of lifeboats carried, and the fact that the *Californian*, so close to the scene of the disaster, failed to respond to *Titanic*'s distress signals. An argument has also been cogently presented that *Titanic* never sank at all, but was a pawn in a massive insurance scam. The myths and legends that quickly accrued in the wake of the disaster obscure the truths of the matter further. Having added this rider, I nevertheless apologize in advance for any faults in this work.

INTRODUCTION

THERE HAD NEVER BEFORE been ships quite like the Olympic-class liners built for the White Star Line by Harland & Wolff, and the story of the RMS (Royal Mail Ship) *Titanic*, the second and best known of the three liners of her class built, and her fateful encounter with an iceberg on the night of 14/15 April 1912, is well known. The greatest piece of man-made technology on Earth spent a bare five days at sea before she sank, taking with her the lives of two-thirds of the passengers aboard. Following that dreadful collision, *Titanic* passed from history into myth and legend, a symbol of what can befall humankind's hubris, a poke in the eye for Victorian and Edwardian smugness, and the sense people had then of the omnipotence of man.

The accident has bred dozens of books and several films, and controversy still rages about precisely what could or should have been done to prevent it. But there is another story: the story of how the ship was constructed, and the story of the men and women who built her and sailed her. This is an attempt to tell that story.

When *Titanic* set off from Southampton on her maiden voyage, on Wednesday (the traditional departure day for White Star liners), 10 April 1912, she surpassed even her slightly older sister, *Olympic*, as the largest (by a matter of a few feet), and certainly the most technologically advanced moving object in the world. Developments in the building of liners, especially those destined for the extraordinarily important transatlantic route, progressed in leaps and bounds between the 1880s and the 1940s. *Titanic* and her sisters would be outstripped in a couple of decades, just as they had outstripped their immediate predecessors. If you moored *Titanic* next to the queens of the Atlantic of the 1930s to the 1960s – the *Queen Mary* and the *Queen Elizabeth*, both run by Cunard White Star – she'd seem small by comparison, as both the latter ships were almost twice her tonnage. And if you set her by those ships' successors, the *QE2* (1969–2008) and the *QM2* (from 2004), she'd be dwarfed. *Titanic*'s gross tonnage was 46,328, and in 1912 her cost on completion was £1.5 million. That would be about £400 million in today's money. The *QE2* cost just over £29 million (about £405 million today), and her gross tonnage was 70,327. The recent *QM2* is a monster: costing £460 million, she weighs in at 148,528 tons. She is 1,132 feet long and her beam at the waterline is 135 feet, as opposed to *Titanic*'s dimensions of 882 feet 9 inches and 92 feet respectively.

By the mid-1960s the aeroplane was beginning to take

over from the great liner as the preferred mode of transport, not just for the privileged, but also for the masses, and now it is the privileged who travel on liners for the most part for pleasure. The last passenger ship built by Harland & Wolff was the *Canberra* in 1960.

The ferrying of passengers, from humble emigrants to wealthy tourists, was a fiercely competitive and lucrative business. And the liners constructed to handle the trade were the work of many thousands of people, skilled, semi-skilled and unskilled, whose toil was long, hard and frequently dangerous. For all the technological advancement and sophistication of the Victorian and Edwardian ages, shipbuilding and heavy engineering in general depended upon a massive workforce prepared to put up with conditions that people in the developed world would now blench at. Yet all this was going on just a century ago. In 1909, the year in which *Titanic*'s keel was laid down, three-quarters of the workforce in Great Britain was made up of manual labourers. Harland & Wolff of Belfast, in Northern Ireland, was the greatest shipbuilding concern in the world, and White Star, *Titanic*'s owners, by then a subsidiary of the massive American company International Mercantile Marine (owned by the financier John Pierpont Morgan), was the jewel in that organization's crown. It all came down to business, of course, but the ships had a real, practical purpose, their lines were still graceful, and they had a romantic quality as well.

The story of *Titanic*'s construction is also the story of the individuals who took part in it – 4,500 of them at least, almost one-third of Harland & Wolff's workforce – over exactly three years, not to mention the other workers across Britain who provided everything from bed linen and crockery to dynamos and anchors for this incredibly complex undertaking.

It is to their memory, and to that of those who sailed *Titanic*, that this book is respectfully dedicated.

'Men worked with their brothers, their fathers, uncles, neighbours and friends. While blokes were at the yard, the women would be running the homes; washing, cooking, cleaning, trying to earn money where they could. As for the kids, well, there were schools of sorts, but most hardly went – by the time you were twelve you had to earn your keep and going to school didn't pay a wage. The simple truth back then was that if you had no work you couldn't survive. There was no social security and no National Health Service, and the Poor House beckoned those who couldn't make their way.'

Anonymous present-day Belfast inhabitant

LAUNCH

WEDNESDAY, 31 MAY 1911, Belfast – a warm, sunny day at the end of spring. The great four-funneller *Olympic*, first of her class, had just reached completion and gone on her sea trials prior to embarking on what was to be a twenty-four-year career (interrupted by the First World War, when she saw service as a troop ship) as the last word in luxury on the transatlantic route: Southampton–Cherbourg–Queenstown (now Cobh) on the south coast of Ireland, and thence to New York.

It was also the launch day of her sister *Titanic* – younger by just a matter of months, for the ships had been built virtually in tandem – the Big 'Un, as she was affectionately known by the men and women who built her and supplied her luxuries. Her completed hull – minus engines, boilers, machinery, propellers, funnels and all superstructure – lay ready for transition from land to sea in Slip 3, one of two massive runways especially and expensively constructed for the building of the Olympic class. In fact,

Olympic herself had been launched on the previous 20 October from Slip 2.

Much press attention had been given to the launch of *Olympic*, and it has to be remembered that, at the time, *Titanic* was number two – very similar to, and (to the untrained eye) virtually indistinguishable from, *Olympic*; but the changes envisaged, subtle though they were, already marked a step forward. *Titanic* was a vast ship – 1,000 tons (gross ton register) heavier than *Olympic*, though only a slight 3 inches longer and 6 inches narrower in the beam. She was the biggest and most spectacular boat in the world. The hull as launched weighed roughly 24,360 tons – nothing like her final tonnage – but it was a lot of weight to shift. Laid on precision-crafted wooden blocks, and supported by a forest of shores under the towering Arrol gantry that had cradled her, *Titanic* lay waiting.

Everything had been meticulously planned. *Olympic*'s launch the previous October had gone without a hitch, and the same system was being used today, with shipyard manager Charles Payne in charge of the launch. The great and the good, plus a cohort of envious and competitive Germans and a contingent of the British and international press, travelled early to Harland & Wolff's Queen's Island shipyard in Belfast on the cross-channel steamer *Duke of Argyll*, which had been specially chartered for the occasion.

For a shipyard, for the people involved, the launch of any ship – even a humble tugboat – is an event. In this case, history was again in the making. Many of the workers who had laboured on the construction of *Titanic*'s hull for just over two years since her keel began its laying-down on 31 March 1909 forfeited a day's pay to be present at the launch. Some of the workmen even had tickets of entry – one at least has been preserved, issued to David Moneypenny, a painter and decorator, who would work on the ship's first-class accommodation. But the *Belfast News Letter* of 1 June 1911 described the scene for those still hard at work: 'Gangs of men were engaged in removing the heavy wooden posts which supported the vessel, a powerful ram being also used in the operation. The clanging of hammers was heard all over the ship as the preparations for the launch were developed, but the men using them were for the most part hidden from view. On the deck of the boat the figures of the workers whose duty it was to see to the drag ropes and cables were dwarfed and blurred by the distance which separated them from the people down below.'

Grandstands had been especially constructed on the ship's port side to accommodate the important major players – the people who'd provided the money, the chief designers, the directors both of Harland & Wolff and of the White Star Line, and their families and associates. According to the *Belfast News Letter*, 'Ladies formed a considerable proportion of the aggregate attendance, and even if their picturesque frocks appeared a trifle incongruous when contrasted with the surroundings of the shipyard itself they were unmistakably in harmony with the glow of the soft turquoise sky, from which the piercing rays of the sun descended, making the heat exceedingly trying for those who witnessed the launch.'

For most of the workers, they just had to find whatever vantage point they could. Everybody in those days accepted the status quo – a status quo that would find its echo throughout the design of the ship.

The launch itself was due to take place at 12.15 p.m., and the timing was precise. Around midday, Lord Pirrie, chairman of Harland & Wolff, together with the White Star Line's managing director, John Bruce Ismay, made a final quick tour of inspection. The bearded Pirrie, epitome of the Victorian entrepreneur, and a tough nut beneath his jovial exterior, sported his usual yachting cap, while Ismay wore a more formal bowler. Satisfied, they left the deck and joined their friends and family – the launch happened to coincide with Lady Pirrie's fifty-fifth birthday.

At 12.05 p.m. a red flag was hoisted at the stern of the vessel to warn people to take their places. Five minutes later a rocket was fired, followed by another just one minute before the launch was due to start. Anyone arriving after the first rocket's firing would not be assured of seats in the stands; and after the second rocket, the doors to Slip 3 were closed, the coffer dam securing the slip from the River Lagan was opened, and all was in readiness for *Titanic* to pass from land to water for the first time and – without any formal ceremony of 'christening' – assume her name.

At the appointed time the signal was given and the huge hydraulic launching rams were activated directly beneath the bow of the ship. As the *Belfast News Letter* recorded the following day: 'The ship glided down to the river with a grace and dignity which for the moment gave one the impression that she was conscious of her own strength and beauty, and there was a roar of cheers as the timber by which she had been supported yielded to the pressure put upon them. She took to the water as though she were eager for the baptism, and in the short space of 62 seconds she was entirely free of the ways.' In that time, the ship that had until now been known as 401 became *Titanic*. Her hull slid over great quantities of lubricant – 15 tons of tallow, 5 tons of mixed tallow and train oil, and 3 tons of soap – and reached a launch speed of 12.5 knots. Once in the water, she was quickly close-hauled by attendant tugs, who pulled her up in less than half her length. Then, riding far higher than she would at completion, for she had an extra 22,000 tons to put on, she was taken immediately and without further ceremony to her fitting-out wharf for completion.

Watching her with anxious eyes was an array of closely involved and, to a degree, closely related people. Chief among these were Thomas Andrews, the Pirries' nephew and the ship's principal designer (already, at thirty-eight, an experienced man, having cut his teeth on *Olympic*), and his predecessor, the Right Honourable Alexander Carlisle, Lord Pirrie's brother-in-law and a consultant designer following his retirement from Harland & Wolff in 1910. Local dignitaries included the Lord Mayor and Lady Mayoress of Belfast, Mr and Mrs McMordie, along with many others from the Belfast *nomenklatura*. Also present was John Pierpont Morgan, the ugly and tough owner of the White Star Line, his beetroot nose (he suffered from rhinophyma) like a beacon.

In a crisp way, as soon as the great ship had slid into the water, the crowds drifted off, and within fifteen minutes Slip 3 was empty, save for the workers clearing up. The principal guests remained at the shipyard, lunching at Lord Pirrie's invitation, while yard officials and other visitors attended a lunch at Belfast's Grand Central Hotel presided over by John Kempster, manager of the new-fangled Electrical Department at Harland & Wolff.

Sardines à l'Imperiale	Cailles sur Canapés.
—	Pommes Château.
Consommé Petite	Salade
Marmite	—
—	Macedoine des Fruits
Saumon naturale.	en Gelée
Sauce Mousseline.	—
Concombre.	Foie de Poulet en
—	Lard
Chaudfroid de Volaille	—
en Aspic	Glace Pralinée
—	
Filet de Mouton à la	Dessert
Sargent.	—
Pommes Fridal.	Café
Choufleur.	
—	

By mid-afternoon, the guests from England were sailing back to Liverpool on *Olympic*, unaware, as most of those attending had been, of the one fatality that had marred the day. A shipyard worker, James Dobbins, who was engaged in knocking out the massive wooden shoring beneath the ship's hull to facilitate her run into the water, was hit by a falling piece of timber and trapped beneath it. Workmates managed to drag him clear, but the injuries he'd sustained were mortal, and he died in hospital a few hours later. When the story got out, it led the myths and (retrospective) omens that dogged *Titanic* after her own fatal collision just over ten months later.

PART 1:
LAYING-DOWN
TO LAUNCH

31 MARCH 1909 – 31 MAY 1911

CHAPTER ONE

THE MAIN PLAYERS

To understand why *Titanic* was built at that precise time, how she was paid for and how she was expected to pay her way, it is necessary to do a bit of scene-setting. Employment in heavily industrialized Belfast relied almost exclusively on the shipbuilding industry, though the linen trade also played a leading role. But industry had become very dependent on foreign capital. Britain was still, at the turn of the twentieth century, the centre of an empire and a leading player on the world's economic stage, but it has to be added that even by the 1880s, the USA and Germany had overtaken her in many areas of industry, and the serious money was already in America. A good deal of it was in the hands of one man, John Pierpont Morgan, who had already seen the money there was to be made in the international shipping industry.

In the first decade of the twentieth century alone, over 8 million emigrants from Europe arrived in New York. The vast majority of these people travelled in the lowest deck –

steerage (so called because the rudder control-lines ran through it), or in third class, a later introduction that offered rather more sophisticated amenities, such as individual cabins. These people nevertheless represented a very profitable source of income. At the other end of the scale there were the wealthy – newly rich Americans in particular – making the grand tour of Europe and fulfilling their cultural dreams in Paris and Rome.

Harland & Wolff enjoyed what might be called a special relationship with White Star. The engineering company built all White Star's ships, and with *Titanic*'s launch in 1911 it achieved the record of having produced a greater overall tonnage of ships in one year than any other yard in the world. The company's vast Queen's Island plant had the unusual ability to offer the complete design and construction of a ship, effectively from keel to sofa cushions, though of course many of the fittings and furnishings were constructed elsewhere by specialists in particular fields.

White Star's policy was to prioritize comfort and luxury over speed. The aim was to make passengers feel that they were in a five-star hotel rather than at sea. Nothing was spared to achieve this impression, noted the contemporary writer Frederick Talbot in *Steamship Conquest of the World*:

Nowadays the traveller, when he steps aboard, enters Utopia. He becomes the pampered child of indulgence. The modern leviathan is provided with seven or more decks, but one is spared the tedious climb and descent of the staircase from one to another. The citizen of the floating town presses a button, a grille rolls back to reveal an elevator, and he is whisked to the desired floor.

There are seductive lounges and saddlebag easy-chairs in the smoking room, and a winter garden where a cup of tea or a modest glass of beer appears instantly in reply to demand. Maybe the day is hot, but welcome relief may be had in the cooling, refreshing waters of the swimming bath. The advocate of physical culture will find in the well-equipped gymnasium every facility to keep in the pink of condition. When time hangs heavily on one's hands, and when shuffleboard, quoits and other orthodox games have expended their fascination in the open air upon deck, there is the racquet court, where prowess may be matched against a fellow-traveller, or a welcome companion in a favourite author may be found in the well-stocked library. Even the luxury of a Turkish bath is not denied to its votaries.

When the traveller finally retires to his couch he makes himself snug and comfortable upon a spring mattress beneath a mass of snowy-white linen. A scarcely perceptible movement of the hand clicks a switch to extinguish the electric light, or, if one be an inveterate reader in bed, there is a friendly shaded light at the elbow. Perhaps some refreshment is desired. The push of a button within arm's reach brings a steward to the bedside.

In the morning, upon waking, a few steps bring one to the bathroom to revel in the invigoration of a needle or spraybath. Before the bugle announcing breakfast rings out, a constitutional may be taken on the promenade deck, and a mile can be covered within two or three laps of the vessel.

My lady possesses equal, if not greater conveniences. On the dressing table is a natty device, which, with the turn of a button, enables her to heat the intricate implements for completing her coiffure. Or she may prefer to leave this delicate, though essential, operation to other and more highly skilled hands. Forthwith she seeks the services of the master in hairdressing, manicure and massage.

Then the morning paper is out. The latest doings on terra firma have trickled onto the ship via the wireless telegraph during the night. The news is set up in terse, cold type in the printing department, and is duly printed upon an unpretentious sheet. While enjoying breakfast one may become acquainted with the world's happenings as easily as on shore.

Talbot was, of course, describing the delights awaiting a first-class passenger; but aboard *Titanic* second class was better than first class on many lesser ships, and even third class had facilities that occupants of staterooms (as the cabins were called) would not have enjoyed on land, such as teak fittings, porcelain sinks, running water and – the ultimate luxury – electricity. Some of the lowlier male passengers had no idea how to use a flush lavatory, never having seen one before. There were accidents. And the sophistication of it all was even harder for non-English-speaking travellers. Signs were in English only, and there was only one interpreter aboard, a Mr L. Müller, who must have been kept extremely busy.

The focus on luxury was part of a general marketing strategy. First-class passengers could expect to pay roughly from £100 to £900, the top price being for a parlour suite; but you could get a first-class berth for as little as £30. Second class might cost as little as £12, but could go up to £50. Third class ranged from £3 to £8 at the lower end, and went up to £20. (These prices are one way only.) However, there was often considerable overlap between adjacent classes. Some staterooms could be adapted to serve the class above or below the one originally designated to them, and much depended on both location and size of cabin.

Setting third-class prices relatively high was deliberate company policy, designed to discourage immigrants from central, southern and eastern Europe. These unfortunates were believed to be dirty and even disease-carrying. Higher prices deterred them politely, and the humbler passengers in third class were nevertheless top dogs among their peers on land. It's as well to remember that Victorian and Edwardian class values reached a long way into the twentieth century: it took two world wars to dismantle them.

But to return to the business behind the romance . . . Shipbuilding in Belfast on any significant scale began in 1791 with the arrival from Scotland of William Ritchie, whose first ship, *Hibernia*, was launched the following year. Ritchie's yard saw the beginning of what would rapidly become a thriving industry, attracted to Belfast by natural advantages and a good pool of local labour.

HARLAND & WOLFF

The greatest of the Belfast shipbuilding companies, Harland & Wolff is still very much alive and well, and operating as always in Belfast. It was founded in 1861 when thirty-year-old Edward Harland, who had bought a shipyard from his former employer, Robert Hickson, for £5,000 three years earlier, went into partnership with twenty-seven-year-old Gustav Wolff, his former personal assistant. Wolff also happened to be the nephew of the German-born merchant and financier Gustav Schwabe, who had helped Harland to buy the yard from Hickson. Schwabe himself had moved to Liverpool in 1838, at the age of twenty-five, and he remained based there until his retirement to London, where he died in 1897.

Both he and the younger Gustav came from Jewish ancestry, though their family (from Hamburg) had converted to Lutheran Christianity in 1819. Gustav Wolff had been sent to join his uncle in 1849, and served an apprenticeship with the Mancunian engineering firm Joseph Whitworth, later graduating to work as a draughtsman with another engineering company, Goodfellows. It was through the influence of his uncle that he secured the job as Edward Harland's assistant.

Harland himself was a hard-headed and exigent businessman. Born in Scarborough in 1831, the son of a doctor, he first studied engineering at the Robert Stephenson works in Newcastle-upon-Tyne. (Stephenson was the son of George, the inventor of the pioneering Rocket locomotive.) Harland subsequently left Newcastle for Glasgow, then returned to Newcastle before joining Robert Hickson's Belfast shipyard in 1854. His move into shipbuilding was prompted by meeting Gustav Schwabe during his apprenticeship. Schwabe, who was friendly with Harland's uncle, was financially involved with the Liverpool-based shipping company of John Bibby & Sons, the oldest independently owned shipping line in the world, founded in 1807 and still operating today as the Bibby Line. It was Schwabe who arranged for the young Edward to be employed at J. & G. Thomson Marine Engineering Company in Glasgow, where he rose to be chief draughtsman at £1 a week. He then returned to Newcastle to become manager of Thomas Toward Shipyard at the tender age of twenty-two. It was Schwabe too who encouraged Edward, a year later, to make the move to Hickson's in Belfast.

Once in charge, Harland set about putting the somewhat ailing shipyard's house in order by following a strict, very Victorian management policy. Wages were cut and smoking was banned to avoid the danger of fires and to discourage the workers from slacking. Harland went about his business in a very hands-on manner, equipping himself with a piece of chalk and an ivory ruler that he used to mark any mistakes he noticed in workmanship. One worker remembered that 'he had an all-smelling nose as well as an all-seeing eye. One day he was walking rapidly along, and he suddenly stopped dead and sniffed at a saw-pit. In a flash the trap-door was lifted and there, squatting in the sawdust, was a wizened little man, puffing at a clay pipe.'

How his workforce must have detested him. However, he restored the yard's fortunes and thus ensured continuing employment for those prepared to toe the line and put their shoulder to the wheel. But it wasn't long before this ambitious young man was casting around for ways of founding a shipyard of his own; he was no doubt very alive to the increasing market for new ships and the burgeoning shipping lines that needed them. After some initial frustration, his prayers were answered in September 1858 when Robert Hickson – perhaps at Schwabe's instigation, for, as we've seen, it was Schwabe who put up the money for his protégé to take over the company – wrote to Harland offering him 'my interest and goodwill in the shipyard at the Queen's Island, Belfast . . . for the sum of five thousand pounds . . .'

The timing was good, for recent years had seen a revolution in design and potential thanks to Isambard Kingdom Brunel, the grandfather of modern heavy engineering. Brunel's ship, the *Great Britain*, made of wrought iron, was built in Bristol in 1843 – only fifteen years before Hickson's offer – for the Great Western Steamship Company. The design and construction set a template for all subsequent iron and steel vessels, and the ship's appearance began a revolution in long-distance travel, which rapidly became not only much quicker, but much more predictable.

Brunel had originally intended to design the *Great*

Britain as a paddle-steamer, but quickly changed his plans to embrace the newly invented technology of screw-propulsion, using propellers, which were far more efficient, especially in heavy seas. The *Great Britain* was in fact driven by one iron propeller whose diameter was a massive and daring 16 feet. But that wasn't her only claim to fame. When she was launched in 1843 she was, at about 1,000 feet long, the largest ship afloat, and a third longer than her nearest rival. She was of course the very first ocean-going, screw-driven iron ship. She weighed an unheard-of 1,930 tons, and – significantly – she was designed for the transatlantic luxury trade. She had a crew of 130 and could carry 252 passengers in first- and second-class berths. At first, though, she was not a financial success, because – despite several safe crossings – relatively few people seemed prepared to sail in her. Great Western sold her on to Gibbs Bright in 1846.

It was under the new ownership, and on the much more ambitious Australian run, that she came into her own, redesigned as an immigrant ship and cashing in on the Australian gold rushes from 1851 onwards. Now able to carry 750 passengers in three classes, she made thirty-two voyages in a twenty-four-year career and earned herself the nickname 'the greyhound of the seas'. (She ended up in Port Stanley in the Falkland Islands in the late 1870s, and remained there, more or less a hulk, for almost a century. Then, in 1970, she was restored and taken back home to Bristol, where she remains, as a museum ship.)

The importance of the *Great Britain*'s legacy is clear,

and Harland was one of many who were very quick to spot what Brunel had started. It wasn't long before he was receiving orders from John Bibby (the company in which Gustav Schwabe had an interest), and he quickly built three ships for the line. Bibby promptly ordered six more in 1860.

After Gustav Wolff became a partner in 1861 and the firm formally became Harland & Wolff, the two men divided the work profitably between them. Wolff had good connections with Hamburg–Amerikanische shipyard in Germany, and Harland, who initially undertook design, created wider ships with flatter bottoms on the box-girder principle in order to increase capacity. The American Civil War of 1861–5 provided useful clients in the Confederate States who wanted steamers fast enough to outrun the Union blockade. The yard prospered, and in 1874 Harland recruited a new partner, William Pirrie, then twenty-seven years old.

Pirrie spent his entire working life at Harland & Wolff, starting there as a fifteen-year-old apprentice in 1862, and rising to become chairman on Harland's death in 1895. He remained in that position until his own death in 1924. A staunch Unionist politically, he had two nephews who became eminent in the public life of Northern Ireland, while a third, Thomas Andrews, became the designer of the Olympic-class liners. Pirrie was the third member of the Harland & Wolff triumvirate, taking over many of the duties, especially of Gustav Wolff, after his elevation to the board. Wolff famously remarked, 'Sir Edward builds the ships, Mr Pirrie makes the speeches, and, as for me, I smoke the cigars.' Harland picked up his baronetcy in 1885. Pirrie was made a viscount in 1921.

> 'The unique position occupied by Messrs Harland & Wolff in the shipbuilding world is due to many causes, but if we were asked to name that which in our opinion was the most potent we should not hesitate to declare for the personal element. Personality has undoubtedly been responsible for the high reputation which the firm possesses . . . not only has it the services of an able and experienced staff, but at the head of affairs is Lord Pirrie, a wonderful personality whose influence pervades the establishment from end to end. On a site without natural advantages, where all the fuel and material required have to be imported, he has raised up a colossal concern which gives employment to between 14,000 and 15,000 men, and pays out in wages over £25,000 a week . . .'
>
> *Syren & Shipping*, 28 June 1911

Alongside these three main players was the chief of design, the Right Honourable Alexander Carlisle (1854–1926). Carlisle joined Harland & Wolff as a sixteen-year-old apprentice and spent his entire career with the yard. Indeed, he was principally responsible for the initial stages of planning the Olympic-class ships.

On Carlisle's retirement, Thomas Andrews took over the design of the Olympic-class liners. He too had begun his career at the shipyard as a teenage apprentice, starting with three months in the joiners' shop, followed by a month with the cabinet-makers, and then two months of manual labour in the yard itself. This rotation continued over an exhaustive and possibly exhausting five years, during which he learnt every aspect of shipbuilding, and culminated with eighteen months in the drawing office. By 1901, having worked his way up the company and gained experience of many departments, Andrews was ready to become manager of the construction works, and in that same year he became a member of the Royal Institution of Naval Architects. Six years later he was managing director in charge of the Harland & Wolff drafting department, and at thirty-four was experienced enough to play a major role in the company's latest and most ambitious venture: the Olympic-class liners.

With great passion and attention to detail, he worked on the designs for the ships from 1907 onwards, right up to the moment of *Titanic*'s departure from Southampton on Wednesday, 10 April 1912. He sailed in her, still making notes for improvements, and on 14 April declared that he believed her to be 'as nearly perfect as human brains can make her'. A matter of hours later, not long after midnight, having inspected the damage caused by the collision with the iceberg, Andrews was telling Captain Edward Smith that *Titanic* would sink within two hours. He was active in conducting passengers to lifeboats, and the story goes that he was last seen staring at the painting *Plymouth Harbour* by Norman Wilkinson, which hung above the fireplace in the first-class smoking room. He went down with the ship he'd designed. It was just two months past his thirty-ninth birthday.

THE WHITE STAR LINE

The White Star Line of Boston Packets, to give it its full title, had a very close, even symbiotic, association with Harland & Wolff. Founded in Liverpool in 1845 by John Pilkington and Henry Threlfall Wilson, its first line of business was ferrying eager immigrants to the goldfields of Australia. This trade was a mother-lode in its own right. In a single month in 1853, for example, no fewer than 32,000 hopeful prospectors left Liverpool for Australia, and in the three years following the discovery by Edward Hammond Hargraves of a goldfield near Bathurst, New South Wales, the population of the southern continent leapt from about 430,000 to well over three times that number.

The White Star fleet initially consisted of chartered sailing ships, among which was RMS *Tayleur*, the largest ship of its day – 230 feet long, 40 feet in the beam, and 1,750 tons. She was wrecked in January 1854 on her maiden voyage out of Liverpool, and her demise was due partly to her crew being inexperienced – of 71 men, only 37 were trained, and 10 could speak no English – and partly to the fact that her iron hull threw her compasses off kilter, so she lost her bearings and foundered in a fog just off Lambay Island, 5 miles from Dublin Bay. In a sinister nod towards *Titanic*'s fate, her rudder was small in relation to her tonnage, and other design and management faults contributed to her tragic destiny. Lifeboats began to be clumsily launched, and as the first smashed on the rocks, attempts to let down others were abandoned. Luckily, the ship was so close to land that the crew was able to topple a mast landward to form a bridge along which the passengers clambered to safety. This was White Star's first worrying knock-back.

But the company flourished, purchased an increasing number of ships, and took on a third partner in the form of James Chambers, Wilson's son-in-law. The fierce rivalry that had existed between White Star and James Baines's Black Ball Line simmered down, and the two lines ended up working in a kind of partnership, to the extent of leasing ships to one another as and when the need arose. The original ships were clippers, constructed of iron and wood, and these, especially after the advent of Brunel's *Great Britain*, soon became obsolete.

Then, in about 1863, a twenty-five-year-old shipping entrepreneur called Thomas Ismay (the unusual surname derives from the French Esmé), who'd already spent five years as partner in a modest firm of shipbrokers, founded his own company, T. H. Ismay and Co., in Liverpool. It grew fast, and a few years later the by-now-wealthy Ismay was buying shares in White Star. Pilkington had retired in 1861 to pursue other business interests, and in time the successful line he had co-founded merged with both Black Ball and the Eagle line, but the venture was unhappy and short-lived. Wilson too left White Star as an active partner, though he continued to acquire ships for the original line and retained 51 per cent of the stock. Meanwhile, White Star had inaugurated an Indian route and purchased its first steamer, *Royal Standard*. This turned out to be a poor investment as, with a top speed of just 6–8 knots, she could be outstripped by sailing clippers. Among the most famous of these, though not built until 1869, was the *Cutty Sark*, a tea clipper, which remained in service until 1922. She wasn't by any means the last fast sailing ship to be built commercially either.

White Star's fortunes took a turn for the worse when the company's bank, the Royal Bank of Liverpool, went under in 1867, leaving the company with debts of £527,000 (about £34 million today). The line had expanded too fast and many of its ships were either obsolete or worked out. Meanwhile, a rival had taken centre stage in the form of the British & North American Royal Mail Steam Packet Company, founded in 1840 by the Nova Scotian Samuel Cunard, and later to assume his name. There was no lack of other rivals either, especially on the growing transatlantic route.

By now Henry Wilson was on the brink of ruin, and, with his partners and fellow shareholders, only too happy to sell White Star to the then thirty-year-old Thomas Ismay for £1,000. Ismay immediately set about replacing the old ships he'd inherited with new ones, renaming the business the Oceanic Steam Navigation Company (OSNC), and concentrating on the transatlantic route. America was opening up and needed people. During and in the wake of the great Irish famine of 1845–52, for example, up to 2 million people left Ireland for a better life elsewhere, principally in the USA.

Ismay began with a capitalization of £400,000 and £1,000 in shares, of which he retained a controlling interest. With a colleague and friend, William Imrie Jr, he also formed Ismay, Imrie & Co. as a subsidiary of OSNC. Under this arrangement, the steamers of the line were run by Ismay under the White Star banner, and the sailing ships by Imrie under the name of North Western Shipping. Ismay also attracted two other major shareholders, Edward Harland and Gustav Wolff, whose shipyard was already attaining a worldwide reputation. This interconnection led to a very useful partnership: White Star commissioned its first sail-assisted steam-liner, *Oceanic*, in 1869. She was put into service two years later. From now on, a business pattern was established. Harland & Wolff would design and build ships for White Star to the highest possible specifications, and then add a fixed percentage to the overall production cost, which percentage constituted their fee. The overall deal, beneficial to both parties, was mutual exclusivity. It is not surprising that our friend Gustav Schwabe had a hand in all this. He and his nephew had had an informal meeting with Ismay, in the course of which Schwabe had simply offered to put money into Ismay's business if he undertook to have his ships built by Harland & Wolff. As we've seen, the first order went through in 1869.

WHITE STAR LINE SAFETY REGULATIONS

Safety was a high priority on Ismay's ships. Among the regulations he painstakingly drew up in about 1870 are the following:

- Watches must be equally divided, no ship shall ever be left without an officer on deck. No officer . . . is to leave the deck while his watch is still in play; first and second officers are never to give up their watch except under clear weather and open sea, at which time they may be relieved by third and fourth officers for their meals. They may also be relieved by the Commanding Officer.
- Watch in dock, Liverpool: an officer to be on deck at all times.
- Watch in dock, abroad. Always to be an officer on deck and at the spar deck, along with two quarter-masters.
- Junior officers must exert themselves to aid naviga-tion of the vessel, and must use solar and stellar observation, both for correction of the compass and to ascertain the position of the vessel.
- Nearing land and heaving the lead, a wide berth is to be given to land and islands. When nearing land take frequent cross-bearings . . . to make sure of the vessel's course. Should weather be unsuitable then

engines should be eased and if necessary stopped. In
fog the steam whistle should be blown and the condition of the weather logged in the log-book.
- Boats, firehouse, pumps etc: A crew to be appointed
to each boat and all tackling to be kept in good order
and ready for immediate service. Exercises are to be
practised regularly and all firehouse and pump
stations are to be kept in working order . . . All crew
is to be properly trained in case of fire or accident.

Concentrating on comfort and safety rather than
speed, Ismay had identified a niche: many of the liners
crossing the Atlantic carried passengers on a one-way trip:
the emigrants. Many shipowners cashed in on a boom trade
and packed as many people on board as they could. The
emigrants were almost exclusively poor workers, and the
conditions they travelled in were dangerous and uncomfortable to say the least. Some owners importing cattle
from America merely hosed down their ships after arrival at
their home ports and reloaded them with emigrants for the
return trip. But Ismay had a longer vision. Early on, White
Star had become a pioneer in offering decent third-class
accommodation on its ships alongside the far more luxurious first and second classes, though of course the
three groups of passengers seldom crossed into each other's
territory, and then only from first to second by choice
or from curiosity. The Oceanic-class liners of the 1870s

could each carry up to 1,000 passengers in third class.

Oceanic's completion was quickly followed by that of three sister ships – *Atlantic*, *Baltic* and *Republic*. Like other companies of the time, White Star established a common theme for the names of its ships, in this case having them end in '-ic'. It also adopted new livery: buff-coloured funnels topped with black (where the soot would discolour them) and black hulls edged with white. Its flag was a broad red, twin-tailed pennant bearing a white five-pointed star.

But the sky wasn't entirely cloudless: *Atlantic*, which had successfully made her maiden voyage to New York in June 1871, struck a submerged rock outcrop off Nova Scotia on her nineteenth voyage from Liverpool, and went down in the early hours of 1 April 1873, losing 562 of the 952 people aboard. Almost all the 117-strong crew survived, but this was the worst loss of civilian life on the transatlantic crossing up to that time. This disaster was not eclipsed until the Norge struck a reef off Rockall in 1904, losing 635 out of 795 lives. But these major disasters were the exception, and most transatlantic crossings, including, ironically, those of the 'cattle-ships', went smoothly.

The first White Star liners – *Oceanic* and the rest – would seem small by today's standards. The first *Oceanic* weighed 3,707 tons, and was 402 feet long by 40 feet 10 inches in the beam, with a speed of 14.5 knots. In 1899 a second *Oceanic* took to the water, and at 17,274 tons was considerably larger than her predecessor. Almost exactly thirty years after the launch of the first quartet, White Star introduced a further four ships into its service. This quartet, launched between 1901 and 1907 and known as the Big Four, marked significant progress. Like *Oceanic II*, they were twin-funnelled, and properly steamers. They were also considerably bigger. *Celtic*, the first of them, weighed 21,035 tons and measured 701 feet in length by 75 at the beam, with a speed of 16 knots. She and her sisters, *Cedric*, *Baltic* and *Adriatic*, were capable of carrying four hundred passengers in first and second class, and up to two thousand in third, as well as 17,000 tons of cargo.

But by the time these ships were being built, White Star was undergoing another transition.

TAKEOVER

Lord Pirrie had succeeded to the managing directorship of Harland & Wolff in 1895 on the death of Edward Harland. He was effectively running the company from that date, and on the definitive retirement of Gustav Wolff in 1906 he also became chairman. In the meantime, thirty-seven-year-old J. Bruce Ismay had taken over the reins of White Star on the death of his father Thomas in 1899. Pirrie and Ismay junior between them inaugurated a new style of management that had to respond to an increasingly competitive transatlantic shipping trade. The competition for customers led to a cut-throat pricing war that forced fares down and, by the beginning of the new century, was cutting profits to the bone and in many cases forcing competitors to trade at a loss – a strategy not too dissimilar to that employed by the airline industry in recent years.

The interdependent White Star and Harland & Wolff found the going hard, but not as hard as some, and White Star managed to pay its shareholders at least 7 per cent a year.

But White Star wasn't invulnerable. The massively wealthy J. Pierpont Morgan, then the world's most powerful financier, was taking more than an academic interest in what was going on, and he had huge funds to back any action he might choose to make.

J. P. MORGAN

Pierpont, as he liked to be called, had entered his father's banking business, joining the firm's London branch at the age of twenty in 1857. He went on to create an empire built on railways and steel, and that included his 'pet' company, International Mercantile Marine, which swallowed as many American and British shipping lines as it could, though Cunard resisted. (It's good to note that the Morgan family wasn't entirely business-orientated, however: Pierpont's uncle James Lord Pierpont was a well-known popular composer, who is probably best remembered today for his 1850s composition 'Jingle Bells'.)

As early as 1893, when Morgan was making the transatlantic crossing himself, a fellow passenger put it to

him that it might be possible to eliminate competition on
the route simply by buying a controlling interest in all the
companies working it. Having established an effective
monopoly, it would then be possible to set realistic fares
that passengers would have to pay if they wanted to travel,
thereby stopping any financial haemorrhage and using at
least some of the profits to improve quality and set standards. Morgan had his hands full with other projects at the
time, but the idea stuck.

Morgan was busy consolidating what was already a
colossal business empire in the USA. He was building up
control of the steel industry there under a consortium
bluntly known as Big Steel. US Steel (the first billion-dollar
company in the world) had interests in everything from
bridge-building to the manufacture of wire and nails, and
as an extension of these it was also gaining control of all
the railway systems in the east. Morgan's ability to buy up
vulnerable companies, reorganize them and turn them
round under his aegis gave birth to a new word – 'morgani-
zation'. In 1896 he was so powerful that he shored up the
US economy by increasing the Federal Treasury reserves
from $38 million to $100 million, the sum needed to put a
stop to a run on the currency.

As the historian Robin Gardiner points out in his stimulating investigation of the possibility that the *Titanic* never
actually sank (see page 270), but was swapped for the
damaged *Olympic* – a virtual twin – in an attempt to
defraud White Star's insurers, Morgan at the time had
'one and a half times as much gold in Fort Knox as the

government of the embryonic superpower'. It was about now that Morgan thought again about the suggestion made to him three years earlier, and he began looking towards the transatlantic shipping trade. To control that, he had to turn his attention to Europe. Europe had already experienced his large-scale, almost rapacious, acquisition of its art, but that was in the nature of a financial sideline compared with the money to be made from a buy-out of its shipping lines. But in one important sense, those very shipping lines needed intervention to sort them out. Competition was driving them into the ground.

Morgan's first target was the Hamburg-based HAPAG line (Hamburg–Amerikanische–Paketfahrt Aktien Gesellschaft), but although they trailed their coat a little, they weren't interested in his overtures. Kaiser Wilhelm II, though, was envious of Great Britain's international dominance, and dreamt of Germany taking the central role on the world's stage. Wilhelm, a grandson of Queen Victoria, had a love-hate relationship with Britain: he admired her way of managing the parts of the world she controlled with a minimum of violence and a maximum of exploitation, and he wanted to emulate this to the extent of having an empire of his own.

The Germans had their own ambitious plans for the maritime market, and their shipyards were gearing up to produce ships that would rival and outstrip Britain's. They did not want, or need, foreign interference or finance. Morgan had no better luck with the other major German shipping line, Norddeutscher–Lloyd. He therefore turned his attention to British targets, where there were plenty of rich pickings. Quite apart from shipping, he even tried to set up a rival system in competition with the London Underground – but in this, to his fury, he was frustrated.

He started by buying a handful of small companies with ease, but when he then approached Cunard, he found himself stonewalled. Cunard, with its fast ships offering reasonable fares and reasonable comfort, could fend for itself, thanks to the help of a government loan of £2.6 million, intended to be spent on two new liners and conditional upon Cunard's not selling up to the Americans for at least twenty years. But White Star was feeling the pinch both from Cunard and from the Germans, despite a good year in 1900, which was the result of transporting troops to the battlefields of the second Boer War (1899–1902). Morgan was habitually aggressive in the manner of his acquisitions, and had the funding to make offers that were hard to resist if he saw an ultimate profit despite paying over the odds at the outset. He therefore made White Star an offer based on their profits for the exceptional year of 1900. The offer was worth ten times those profits.

But Bruce Ismay, for the moment, did resist. He didn't want to lose his independence, and White Star, like Cunard, had some state support to fall back on. But the great *éminence grise* of the British shipping industry, Gustav Schwabe, had died in 1897, so the intelligent business muscle was no longer there to support or advise him.

Morgan's response, using the lines he'd already acquired, was to apply pressure by lowering fares. White

Star, as Michael Davie points out in *The Titanic: The Full Story of a Tragedy* (see page 270), found third-class fares drop to a ridiculous £2. Morgan had the financial power to lose money in order to crush rivals; short-term loss meant nothing in terms of the ultimate goal. Matters were brought to such a pass that White Star could not afford to commission any more new ships from Harland & Wolff.

A sticking-point had arrived. Crucial to its resolution was the attitude of William Pirrie. As the hard-headed boss of Harland & Wolff, Pirrie felt no compunction to stand by Ismay. He supported Morgan's bid, well aware that his own shipyard would stand to profit by the takeover. Outmanoeuvred and under pressure from his shareholders, Ismay saw that he couldn't carry on alone. White Star therefore folded, and Morgan took over in 1902, having paid $10 million – way above its market value. Morgan was additionally prepared to give assurances that the White Star ships would be crewed by British nationals, retain their status as reserves for the Royal Navy, and could be requisitioned should the need arise. (This was an astute move, since Kaiser Wilhelm II was already beginning to show signs of belligerence, despite the strained diplomatic efforts of his uncle, Edward VII of England, who succeeded Victoria in 1901.)

White Star thus became part of Morgan's International Navigation Company of Philadelphia, which in 1902 changed its name to International Mercantile Marine (IMM), at the same time raising its capital from $15 million to an immense (for the time) $120 million.

IMM rapidly absorbed several other British shipping lines.

In the end, Morgan only partially realized his ambition, and ended up with about 30 per cent of the transatlantic trade, but that was still a handy slice of the cake. Nevertheless, the big conglomerate needed a steady and experienced hand at the tiller if it were to prosper, and Morgan's choice for running IMM fell on Bruce Ismay. But White Star and its ships were now effectively American-owned, and there were Americans on its board of directors.

Ismay needed some persuading to take the job. Perhaps he felt that Morgan had overreached himself, that the cartel would fall apart, and that he would eventually regain control as his own master. But Morgan assured him that he would have autonomous control over everything 'except finance'. However back-handed this might sound, Morgan sugared the pill by giving further assurances that, as Michael Davie records, he would 'make available a private line of cash, which would be greatly to the advantage of both White Star and Harland & Wolff' – in effect, offering Ismay total control of his company. Pirrie no doubt added his own persuasive words.

This wasn't completely string-free, however. By 1904, Morgan had made a heavy personal stake in IMM – upwards of $2.5 million – and his shareholders had put up $50 million. He was disinclined to invest any more of his own money before he saw a return, and in a letter placed a three-year limit to his bounty, dating from 1 January 1904. This caveat was not lost on Ismay, but he was a capable man who didn't want to lose the baby with the bathwater.

Seeing that he really had no room to manoeuvre, he accepted Morgan's offer and became chairman and managing director of International Mercantile Marine in February 1904. IMM controlled the Oceanic Steam Navigation Company and Ismay, Imrie & Co., together with four other lines: Dominion, Red Star, Leyland and Atlantic.

Ismay managed the company with a sure hand, fending off pleas for more cash from an impatient Pirrie, and doing his best to cope with the competition from HAPAG, Norddeutscher–Lloyd and Cunard. But it wasn't easy. Cunard had state backing to build two huge new liners, which, as fashion and custom dictated, had four funnels for greater élan and cachet (though the fourth acted only as a ventilator). The first was the *Lusitania*, launched in June 1906 and weighing over 31,500 tons; the second, built at a different yard, was the *Mauretania*, launched on 20 September 1906 at a little under 32,000 tons. These ships set a new benchmark: they were fast, having a top speed of over 26 knots. They also set new standards of safety and comfort. People loved them. Passengers flocked to them. White Star needed to respond to woo custom back.

Having the might of Morgan's empire behind it, White Star didn't drag its feet. The story goes that Pirrie invited Ismay to dine with him at his house in Belgravia, London, and over dinner floated the idea of building two liners for White Star that would be bigger and better than the Cunarders. The idea of building three-funnellers was broached as only three funnels were actually needed, but this was later rejected. It would be the Germans who, soon after the demise of *Titanic*, introduced three-funnelled liners, and these would become the norm for the next few decades. Once the initial strategy had been agreed, Harland & Wolff began work on the design, and by the summer of 1908 senior executives from White Star were invited to Belfast to view the plans. The drawings were for 'Number 400', as this – the first of the two new liners – would be the shipyard's four hundredth product. Only after launching would it become *Olympic*. Its engineering, construction and design details were later adopted for the second liner, *Titanic*, but with improvements – a redraft, if you like.

The designs were not revolutionary, and in some ways could even be called conservative. The straight stem was relatively new, and bemoaned by traditionalists, who would miss the yacht-like prows of older ships that were capable of carrying a figurehead. The stern was elegantly elliptical and schooner-rigged.

The devil was in the detail, and design innovation concentrated on passenger accommodation, which was intended to emphasize opulence. As in the Cunarders, the first-class dining saloon would be lit by a vast glass dome; there would be a gymnasium, a squash court, a Turkish bath and a swimming pool. There would be electric lifts to all necessary decks, not only for first class, but second as well. Power and speed were less important than style and luxury. The Cunarders were powered by turbines, a recent invention pioneered by the engineer Charles Parsons, who had built his first one in 1887, though the principle had been discovered by French engineers as early as 1828. Turbines were more powerful and more economical than the reciprocating, or piston, engines used hitherto (and still in use), but for their new liners, Harland & Wolff opted for a combination of two reciprocating engines to drive the port and starboard propellers, and a turbine aft of them in the hull to drive a central propeller tucked in behind the rudder, which would be driven by the steam created by the other engines. The proposed new ships wouldn't be as fast as the Cunarders – they'd have a speed of about 21 knots – but they'd be far more stylish and half as big again as their rivals. It was a bold ploy. To raise the money to build Number 400, White Star launched a new share issue to the value of £1.5 million – precisely the amount, as it turned out, that it cost to build each of the Olympic-class liners. Morgan's imprimatur ensured the issue was filled.

Some corners were cut. Alexander Carlisle had wanted sixty-four lifeboats, but this was far in excess of Board of Trade requirements, and the number was reduced in stages, first to forty-eight, then thirty-two, and finally, in 1910, to sixteen. With good reason, and despite the two disasters that had befallen White Star ships in the nine-teenth century, everyone had faith in the seaworthiness of the new leviathans. However, no one took into account that they would each weigh around 46,000 tons. Board of Trade lifeboat regulations, last revised in 1894, were based on a tonnage of 10,000, with a proportionate passenger capacity.

But a new surge of confidence swept through White Star and Harland & Wolff: the all-but sister companies felt themselves to be on the verge of a new adventure and a new lease of life.

CHAPTER TWO

SISTERS AND RIVALS

To place *Titanic* in her context, it makes sense to look at her sister ships, whether they belonged to her own stable or to rival companies. The Olympic-class trio (*Olympic*, *Titanic* and *Britannic*) weren't built in any kind of limbo, and now we have understood the financial grounding and the commercial motivation that made them possible, it's worth looking at them in the context of their competition.

The hundred years between about 1850 and 1950 saw the most extraordinary progress in shipbuilding, but the peak was undoubtedly in the middle of that period. While Tyneside and Clydeside boasted a fair number of major shipbuilding companies, there is little doubt that at the time of building the Olympic-class trio, Belfast – thanks to Harland & Wolff – wore the crown. As the *Belfast News Letter* reported on 21 October 1910:

The *Oceanic*, with her 17,000 tons . . . rode the waves to usher in the twenty-thousand tonners . . . Germany, however, then stepped in in the matter of speed and also in size, and held it [sic] until the *Lusitania* and the *Mauretania* were built . . . Theirs is the thirty-thousand-tonner period, and, so far as known ambitions go, they are threatened with no rivalry in speed. But the thirty-thousand tonner must now take second place; the *Olympic* ushers in the forty-thousand-ton period, and her sister ship, the *Titanic*, will be launched from the sister slip on the Queen's Island, a few months hence. So the pride of place, for everything in mercantile marine construction but speed, has come back to Belfast with a margin of advance that marks another great upward stride in mercantile marine construction.

As explained in Chapter 1, J. Pierpont Morgan's money provided both the means and the stimulus to compete with the giant Cunarders, and White Star was wise to place its emphasis on luxury rather than speed. However, it should be remembered that the Olympic class, while bigger than anything else afloat, did not break any boundaries in terms of design. It could be argued that the Cunarders, *Lusitania* and *Mauretania*, were more progressive designs.

Titanic's slightly older sister, *Olympic*, was the only one to survive for more than two and a half years. Despite occasional accidents and collisions, she earned the nickname 'Old Reliable' and stayed in service until 1935, by which time she'd become simply too old-fashioned for passengers of the day. People wanted en-suite bathrooms by then, and except for the top-whack first-class state-rooms, the liners of *Olympic*'s day just didn't offer such facilities. On the other hand, elegance began to give way to the gin palace. Just compare the *Queen Elizabeth* with the *QE2*, especially after the latter's refit, to give a recent example. But, to be fair, the staterooms of the great four-funnellers of a century ago do seem cramped and crowded to the modern eye, and the styles of decor, so chic then, look claustrophobic. There are plenty of photographs, but to get a real flavour of what things were like, go to the White Swan Hotel in the beautiful city of Alnwick, Northumberland, where some of the furnishings come from the 1935 auction of *Olympic*'s effects; or visit the Southampton Maritime Museum, where you can see Charles Wilson's famous carved wooden clock frame, 'Honour and Glory Crowning Time', which featured on *Olympic* and also possibly on *Titanic*; or go to Belfast, where artefacts made too late to be installed in *Titanic* for her maiden voyage can also be seen.

OLYMPIC

Laid down on 16 December 1908, *Olympic* was launched on 20 October 1910. Her hull was painted light grey for the occasion, the usual practice at the time, since the colour enhanced the lines of the ship in black-and-white photography, an advantage to Harland & Wolff's official photographer, Robert Welch, and his colleague William Green.

Olympic took her maiden voyage to New York on 14 June 1911. Her gross tonnage at 'birth' was 45,324, increased to 46,358 after 1913, and to 46,439 after 1920, the weight gain being due to new fixtures and fittings and improved safety measures. Like her tragic sister, she was driven by two four-cylinder, triple-expansion reciprocating engines each at 15,000 whp and a low-pressure turbine driving a centre propeller. These engines could produce a cruising speed of 21.7 knots, and a top speed of 23. She used 650 tons of coal in a twenty-four-hour day. The ship had a maximum capacity of 2,435 passengers, and was built virtually in tandem with *Titanic*, sharing designers Alexander Carlisle and (principally) Thomas Andrews.

To accommodate the building of such vast ships, it was necessary for Harland & Wolff to expand the size of its slipways. Three existing slips were adapted to make two larger ones, in which *Olympic* and *Titanic* were built side by side, to a large extent from the same plans. Slips 2 and 3 were excavated in 1907, amid filthy and primitive working conditions, but enthusiastically driven forward by William Pirrie, Bruce Ismay and, of course, Morgan. The new slips were dredged to a depth of 50 feet – an increase of 35 feet – and their floors were covered with concrete to a depth of 4½ feet.

Thomas Andrews sailed with *Olympic* on her maiden voyage, together with his 'guarantee crew' of eight experts, who were there to take care of any snags that might occur. This highly skilled group included a joiner, a draughtsman, three fitters, a plumber and two electricians. Although they were given passenger rather than crew accommodation (indeed, the draughtsman and the electrician – theirs being elite trades – travelled first class with Andrews), they were nevertheless classified as crew. Doubtless their presence in passenger accommodation was to ease Andrews' access to them. A similar crew would travel with him on *Titanic*, and all would go down with the ship.

Olympic was more economical than her Cunard rivals – her daily coal consumption was 250–350 tons less than that of the *Lusitania* and *Mauretania*, which consumed about 1,000 tons – but of course she was slightly slower. A cynic might have observed that she was also accident-prone, despite the good safety record of her captain, Edward Smith, who later took command of *Titanic*, having handed over *Olympic* to Captain Herbert Haddock.

Olympic's first accident was a collision with HMS *Hawke*, a navy cruiser, off the Isle of Wight in September 1911. She damaged a propeller shaft and flooded two of the watertight compartments, but managed to get back to Southampton under her own steam. The Royal Navy put the blame on White Star, claiming that *Olympic*'s vast displacement had created a suction effect that had drawn the *Hawke* towards her, but the accident's true cause is still debatable. The damage from the collision was reparable, but the financial consequences were important, as the repair work meant that *Titanic*'s construction schedule was delayed.

In the wake of the *Titanic* disaster, *Olympic* was refitted to encompass higher safety standards. Some water-tight bulkheads were raised to B-deck level, and enough lifeboats were fitted for the ship's whole complement. Even so, in late April 1912 there was a strike of the ship's firemen, who didn't think the collapsible extra lifeboats, bought second-hand, were seaworthy. Matters came to an ugly head when White Star preferred a charge of mutiny against the strikers, but the Plymouth court dismissed the charge, and in mid-May *Olympic* resumed her sailing schedule. Later on, the collapsibles were replaced with proper wooden boats.

Although *Olympic* remained in passenger service for part of the First World War, the Germans' declaration that merchant ships, including passenger ships, would be fair game for their U-boats (the *Lusitania* was sunk by *U-20* on 7 May 1915) meant that few travellers were willing to risk the transatlantic route. White Star wanted to lay up *Olympic* for the duration of the war, but she was requisitioned as a troop transport by the Royal Navy in September 1915, refitted, armed and renamed HMT (His Majesty's Transport) *2810*. Famously, she sank a U-boat (*U-103*) in May 1918 – the only example of a merchant ship sinking an enemy warship in that war. She resumed her name and civilian duties late in 1919 and continued in service until 1935, the year following White Star's merger with Cunard. *Olympic* was definitively broken up in 1937 at Ward's yard in Inverkeithing, Scotland.

BRITANNIC

The third and largest of the trio, at 48,158 gross tons, *Britannic* (which some sources say was originally to be named *Gigantic*) was laid down at the end of November 1911 and launched towards the end of February 1914. She was put into service just before Christmas 1915, but never saw civilian use. In fact, she was requisitioned by the navy as a hospital ship (HMHS *Britannic*) and didn't last a year – she hit a mine in the Aegean in November 1916, and sank with the loss of thirty lives. Luckily, she wasn't carrying any wounded. Safety improvements meant that six of her fifteen watertight bulkheads had been raised to the level of B deck, and that she carried massive lifeboat davits, big enough to lower boats on the opposite side to where they were slung. Alas, these sophisticated improvements didn't help on the day of her sinking: two lifeboats were lowered too fast and were sucked into her propellers, which tore the boats and their occupants to shreds. Fortunately, the engines were then stopped and the rest of the ship's complement was able to abandon ship safely. By far the largest Allied ship lost in the First World War, *Britannic*, whose wreck was discovered by the oceanographer Jacques Cousteau in 1975, still lies on the seabed off Kea in the Cyclades.

The only survivor of the entire Olympic family is the tender *Nomadic*. She is currently being restored in Belfast. She, together with her sister *Traffic*, ferried passengers to and from *Titanic* at Cherbourg on the evening of 10 April 1912.

MAURETANIA

'*Maury*', as the *Mauretania* was affectionately known, weighed 31,938 tons, and had a length of 790 feet and a beam of 88 feet. At the time of her maiden voyage in November 1907 she was the largest and fastest ship in the world, and held the Blue Riband for the speediest crossing to New York between 1909 and 1929 (First World War years excepted), and in the opposite direction from 1907 to 1929. Her designer, Leonard Peskett, later sailed on *Olympic* and took copious notes, but the *Mauretania* herself had been built at Harland & Wolff's rivals Swan Hunter and Wigham Richardson on Tyneside. She was powered by the then new Parsons turbine engines, which gave additional speed, though they set up uncomfortable vibrations, which Peskett sought to limit by redesigning the propellers and strengthening *Maury*'s box-girder construction. The *Mauretania* was the first ship to have passenger lifts, a French-style veranda café, classical period interior decor in first class, a grand staircase and a glass cupola – all features copied for the Olympic-class White Star liners.

The *Mauretania* was requisitioned during the First World War as an armed merchantman, but the navy didn't like her much because she was so big and cost so much to run. On the other hand, her high speed meant she could outrun U-boats, so she – like her Cunard sisters and her White Star rivals – was painted with dazzle camouflage inspired by Cubist painting. Later she became a hospital ship and was repainted white, with massive red crosses.

Maury returned to civilian service in September 1919,

was given a refit in 1928, and continued to work until 1934, when she was withdrawn and joined *Olympic* in the queue for the breakers' yard. Her former commander, Arthur Rostron, who had been captain of the modest Cunarder *Carpathia* when it went to the rescue of the stricken *Titanic*, couldn't bear to see her go. And among the passengers who'd loved her was Franklin D. Roosevelt, who wrote a letter protesting at her scrapping. Parts of her survive: her first-class writing room, for example, is now the boardroom of Pinewood Studios.

CARPATHIA

A much smaller ship than *Titanic*, the *Carpathia* was built by Swan Hunter and Wigham Richardson for Cunard at the beginning of the twentieth century. She made her maiden voyage in May 1903, remaining in service until 1918, when she was sunk by a torpedo fired by *U-55* off the east coast of Ireland. Her wreck was discovered by the exploration company Argosy International in 1999, and confirmed by marine archaeologist and best-selling author Clive Cussler in 2000. She weighed 13,555 tons, and had a length of 541 feet, a beam of 64½ feet and a modest speed of 17.5 knots. In her time she made the Liverpool–Queenstown–New York/Boston runs, as well as the Trieste/Fiume–New York runs in winter, carrying in her heyday 2,550 passengers in third class, 200 in second and 100 in first.

The *Carpathia* was sailing from New York to Rijeka on the Croatian coast when she picked up *Titanic*'s distress calls. Captain Rostron, a hero if ever there was one, made haste to reach the stricken super-liner, cutting off hot water and heating in order to put on as full a head of steam as possible. His ship arrived at the scene at 4.00 a.m. on Monday, 15 April.

CALIFORNIAN

Less worthy of praise is the *Californian*, ironically belonging to another of J. Pierpont Morgan's buy-ups, the Leyland Line. The *Californian*, a one-funneller like many of her predecessors, made her maiden voyage on 31 January 1902 and was sunk by a U-boat in the Aegean in November 1915. She was a small ship, displacing 6,223 tons and measuring 447 feet in length by 53 feet at the beam.

Her route was initially Dundee to New Orleans, and she was only 20 miles away from *Titanic* when the distress signals arrived. However, her captain, Stanley Lord, failed to heed the signals. Although he goes down in history as irresponsible, he cannot fully be blamed. Both he and the *Californian*'s radio operator had retired for the night (wireless operators were not required to work a twenty-four-hour shift at the time) when *Titanic* sent out her first distress call, so there was no one awake on the ship to hear her calls for help. Lord was also ill-advised by his junior officers: Lord said he was told of one rocket and asked if it had been a company signal; his second officer said he didn't know.

Whether it was confusion that led the captain and officers of the *Californian* to ignore *Titanic*'s distress rockets and dismiss them as company signals is still a matter under debate. Nevertheless, if he had given the situation the benefit of the doubt, the major part of the tragedy would have been averted. The *Californian* belatedly joined *Carpathia* in quest of survivors, but only at 8.00 a.m. on the following morning. By then, of course, it was far too late.

GERMAN COMPETITION

More competition for the Olympic-class trio came from the Germans, who were eager to assert their supremacy wherever they could. They were nothing if not good engineers, but, with unfortunate timing, their big ships entered the market just before the First World War, and became booty for the Allies afterwards. They were, however, the first of the three-funnellers, setting a new benchmark and a new fashion. The funnels of the German ships were massively tall and hugely impressive.

The predictably named *Imperator* (later the British *Berengaria*) was, at her entry into service in June 1913, the world's biggest ship, at 52,117 tons, until she was eclipsed by her sister *Vaterland* (later the American SS *Leviathan*). *Imperator* could carry 942 third-class passengers, and another 1,772 in steerage in dormitory-style berths: emigration with a vengeance.

The Germans' hegemony was, however, short-lived after their vainglorious first attempt at European domination. The French opted for smaller size but greater elegance. The *France* was their only four-funneller, but a baby at 23,666 tons. Her maiden voyage began a week after the *Titanic*'s. What trepidation her passengers must have felt.

The drive to build bigger and better ships dominated the first two decades of the twentieth century, and the Olympic class remains the apogee of those efforts.

CHAPTER THREE

PORTS AND PREPARATIONS

BELFAST

To further understand *Titanic* and the people who built her it is important to visualize what Belfast was like in the first decade of the twentieth century, what the work opportunities were for 'ordinary' people, what underpinned the simmering political situation, and, above all, what Belfast's status was as a highly specialized industrial capital.

In 1911 there were rumblings of revolution in the air. The Siege of Sidney Street had taken place in January in the East End of London, with Home Secretary Winston Churchill arriving in person as the police shot it out with Russian anarchists armed with 'broomhandled' Mauser pistols; and the abortive revolution in Russia of 1905 had not disappeared from people's minds, in particular the minds of politically motivated workers. But to counter this, opportunities for work were expanding, not least in Belfast.

Things had happened fast. Belfast had started life as a medieval castle built on a strategic headland. It became a town proper only at the beginning of the seventeenth century, when it was developed by its English owner, Arthur Chichester. By the beginning of the nineteenth century the still-rural Belfast had a population of about 25,000, and this increased to only 70,000 over the next fifty years. But by 1911 the population had grown enormously, to nearly 400,000. The advent of industry, and especially the shipping industry, was the reason for this. As mentioned in Chapter 1, William Ritchie established a shipyard for wooden windjammers in 1791, and the first iron ship, the *Countess of Caledon*, a Lough Neagh steamer, was constructed there by boilermakers William Coates & Son in 1838.

Belfast was now the biggest city in Ireland – far bigger than Dublin, which still based its economy on land and trade – and this was in a country whose population had for half a century been in decline as a result of the potato famine and consequent emigration, largely to the USA. The scale on which the city was booming eclipsed even its rivals in northern England, but it had its own internal tensions. Arthur Chichester had peopled his settlement with English and Scots, all Protestant and Presbyterian. The native Irish, all Catholic, lived mainly to the west of the town. Throughout the first two centuries of its life, Belfast was both radical and democratic. Religious tension was unknown, despite earlier attacks on the Catholic Irish by the likes of the Elizabethan explorer Sir Walter Raleigh and the Puritan politician Oliver Cromwell. (But the history was to add up, of course, and the way the English dealt so brutally with the Great Famine of the mid-nineteenth century scarcely helped to create goodwill.)

By the time of the first insurrection against English rule in 1798, Belfast had already set foot on the path that would lead to its commercial future, and the production of linen (on the Antrim side of town) and the production of ships (on Queen's Island) were establishing themselves as its defining industries. Indeed, heavy investment in the recently perfected mechanized spinning wheels would quickly efface the cottage-industry handicraft of the rural vicinity, and by 1900 the linen industry would be employing 35,000 workers within the city.

Shipbuilding at the time did not employ as many workers as linen, but that would soon change. Throughout the nineteenth century the shallow waters of the city were systematically dredged, and by the time Harland & Wolff came into its own, the depth of the waters of the River Lagan and the Musgrave Channel meant that larger ships than ever before conceived could be built and floated with ease.

'Managing the massive workforces of the industrial age required rigid structures, strict discipline and constant supervision. Time was money and men were machines. The thousands of men who entered the shipyard each day were broken down into manageable crews, each led

> by a foreman, or 'hat'. 'Hats', named after the bowlers
> they wore, which defined their status, ran their crews
> with rods of iron, barking their instructions through
> megaphones, constantly on the alert for shoddy work-
> manship, and with the power to dock wages for any
> slacking.'

But shipbuilding and linen were not the only industries to flourish. Manufacturing chemical dyes,
rope-making, distilling and tobacco curing followed, and as
the town prospered, so it grew. It quickly became a place of
international importance, and the buildings that sprang up
reflected this. In 1888, Belfast ceased to be a mere town
and was formally incorporated as a city. The boom attracted
tens of thousands of rural Irish Catholics in search of
higher wages and a more predictable income than the
land could afford. In 1784, Catholics made up 8 per cent
of the town's population. By 1911 that percentage had
trebled.

The Belfast bourgeoisie lived in the districts centred
on Malone Road and Botanic Avenue. By contrast, the
shipyard workers lived in crowded redbrick terraces close
to Queen's Island. But alongside the class divide existed a
sectarian divide. Prejudice – blinkered, self-serving and
divisive as it was and continues to be – bore its usual fruit.
Orange Day (12 July), marked by a Protestant march to
honour the victory of William of Orange over the Catholic
James II at the Battle of the Boyne in 1690, saw sectarian

battles even in the early decades of the nineteenth century, and by the 1850s they had become unmanageable. Territorial battle-lines were drawn up: the Catholics occupied the southwest of the city and left most of the rest to the economically dominant Protestants. And there were further frontiers – separate schools, for one thing; and a division of labour, for most of the Catholic workers were unskilled, or at least excluded from skilled employment. It was small wonder that the Protestants, out of self-interest, would associate themselves with the Unionist cause, and that the Catholics, wishing to be part of the socio-religious majority of Ireland in the hope of a fairer deal, joined the Nationalists. By 1911, the year of *Titanic*'s launch, Dublin was still the centre for the British administration of Ireland; but the focus and fulcrum for loyalism to the Crown was Belfast, vastly more important in every way, but above all economically, than any other conurbation in Ireland. All other arguments apart, it is no wonder that Great Britain didn't want to let Belfast go to any Irish Republic.

So, we have a copybook Victorian boom town – smug, materialistic and rich. Belfast had electric trams and big new public buildings in the various neo-Gothic, quasi-Greek, vaguely Palladian and over-iced Georgian styles favoured by the Victorians. Underneath the affluent appearance, social differences simmered. The middle-class suburbs grew and prospered, fed by the tramway, but the working class, which powered the city, found that its housing scarcely increased at all. Despite the prosperity, the gulf between wealthy and poor increased, and the living standards of the poor (predominantly Catholic) actually declined. In the midst of this, the Protestant skilled working class and the Unionist leaders of industry (including Harland & Wolff), mutually threatened by what they saw as the spectre of Irish Nationalism, drew together against the prospect of Home Rule.

Titanic set off from Southampton on her maiden voyage the day before the Third Irish Home Rule Bill came before the Commons on 11 April 1912, and it's worth bearing in mind the political melting-pot that formed the backdrop to her construction. So ludicrous did partisanship become that her alleged (and totally false) ship number, 3909 ON, was deemed to be a code: in mirror image, and with a good dollop of imagination, this cipher could be understood as NO POPE – a sectarian slogan of the time. Paradoxically, *Titanic* herself became a symbol of Unionist hubris.

Even though Belfast was a recognizably modern city, just 5 miles outside it rural life prevailed pretty much as it had a hundred years previously – a world of horse-drawn wheel-less slide-cars, of men fishing from coracles, of humble little shops, of hand-looms worked by men in their own tiny kitchens, of harvest-homes that wouldn't seem unfamiliar to a fourteenth-century serf. The villages, formed of low thatched cottages strung along an unmade main street, hugged the land as if they had grown out of it. But this was a society that hadn't long to live.

Back in Belfast, anything up and coming was in the

hands of the rich. Cars, for example, were hugely fashionable, as was the clothing in which to drive them. A Ford Model T, in production from 1908 until 1927, cost about $550 in 1910 (the equivalent of about £13,500 today), but the price decreased over subsequent years as profits caught up with production costs. For those on more modest incomes, there were bicycles, but in 1910 a new bicycle would set you back £12 – six weeks' wages for a skilled worker. Then there was air travel, still in its infancy, but proved possible in principle, and which in two decades would be properly grown up.

In their limited time off, workers enjoyed the usual recreations of breeding poultry and terriers, whippet racing and social drinking. Given their long and arduous working day, it's a wonder they had the energy to do more than eat and sleep. Harland & Wolff, though, were good employers, paid a fair wage, and treated their workforce strictly but decently. However, Victorian class values still prevailed, as recounted by a former employee: 'Everything was controlled. The bosses kept an eye on everything, every minute of the day. You couldn't sit down without someone shouting at you. It helped create a real us-and-them mentality. If you were a boss you were a part of the system, and if you were a worker, we was all in it together. You have to remember this was tough, dirty, dangerous work, so a bit of spirit was important to help you get through the days.'

Fines were imposed for all sorts of offences – smoking, loafing (idling), and even playing football with rivets. One of the commonest offences was 'boiling can' –

that is, making tea at unauthorized times and in unauthorized places, as for instance when boiling water up on one of the portable rivet furnaces.

Fines were expressed in the Fines Books either in cash terms, or in terms of paid time forfeited. For example, on 9 December 1910 a fitter's assistant called John Henry was fined a quarter of a day's pay for 'dropping links from Gangway No. 401 [i.e. *Titanic*]'. Three days later an apprentice fitter was docked half a day's pay for 'boiling can at 8.10 a.m.' although this was only ten minutes before tea was officially allowed to be brewed, so it's easy to see how strictly the rules were enforced. Bad timekeeping was a frequent offence and cost the offender 2s 6d (the equivalent of about £10 today). Playing cards or football during working hours were similarly punished. An apprentice plater called William Vance was fined 2s 6d on 9 June 1909 for 'destroying hammers shaft'; and an apprentice driller called William Robson was fined 1s on 10 February that year for 'loafing and going down gangway before time'.

'The rules of the yard were absolute, and they covered every aspect of the day. The first morning of course I had to respond to a call of nature and I didn't know where to go, so one of the other apprentices took me to the lavatory block. This was up a sort of spiral staircase and there was a little office at the top with a clerk in it, and he took your number. Everyone had a number, which was stamped on a little piece of wood called "the board", and you kept the board, which was about the size of a cigarette packet but not as thick, in your pocket. The clerk either took the board or took your number. He then explained the rules, which were very simple, and I can remember exactly what he said. He said, you are allowed seven minutes in the forenoon and seven minutes in the afternoon, and that was it. Any extension of that time would either need a doctor's note, or you'd be fined. The term "minutes" came to mean "lavatories", and in fact if you were looking for someone you might be told, he's away to the minutes, and you'd know what was meant.'

Former shipyard worker

'And what of women workers during this time? Let's take a fairly typical example. Elizabeth Sproule was eighteen years old when she married Robert Murphy senior, then an apprentice riveter at Harland & Wolff, on Christmas Eve, 1880. They'd grown up together on the same street, and their first married home was a near-hovel in Murphy's Court, an area so grim that the census people didn't care to visit it. They had at least six children, though three died in infancy, again typical of the time.

A common practice among working men was to take their wages, paid in cash at the end of the week, and make straight for the pubs, where a pint of Guinness cost the equivalent of 2p. Whatever they didn't spend there, and for many that wasn't much, had to pay for food and rent. Elizabeth was lucky – her husband was a teetotaller, so she never had to endure the miseries many other women suffered. Of course, the man of the house always got the lion's share of any food so that he'd have the strength needed for his heavy work at the shipyard. Children got the next portion, and the mother had to make do with whatever was left. In the poorest families the womenfolk were frequently malnourished.

Elizabeth Sproule found work in the linen mills, where women workers dominated, and many took their babies with them. Stories abound of pregnant women walking to the mill, putting in a twelve-hour day, walking home again, giving birth in the night, and going to work with their newborn the next morning. Elizabeth Sproule may have been luckier than some, but it was in the linen mills that she picked up tuberculosis from the foul air, and it killed her in 1897, when she was thirty-five years old.'

At a time when workers' interests were at last being recognized and focused on through the work of the philosophers Karl Marx and Friedrich Engels, it's unsurprising that some workers interested themselves in politics. Others took up literature and the natural sciences. One worker in particular, Robert Bell, was a keen amateur geologist and mineralogist, the discoverer of several species of fossil mollusc, whose contribution to science was such that several examples were named after him.

These, then, were the social and political circumstances in Belfast surrounding *Titanic*'s birth. The city was
like a tectonic plate where the old world met the new, and
the reverberations of that meeting would have a profound
impact.

SOUTHAMPTON

In 1907, White Star implemented a change that had a
serious effect on employment and social structure in
Belfast: it changed its port of departure from Liverpool to
Southampton. Cunard would follow suit after the First
World War.

Southampton had many clear advantages over
Liverpool. For a start, it was a natural deep-water port, and
its double high tides saved ships long and expensive waits
outside the harbour. (The P&O Line and the Royal Mail
Steam Packet Company were already established there.) It
was also far closer to London, with a direct rail link to the
city, and only a short distance from France, where passengers bound for America could be conveniently picked up at
Cherbourg. In addition, it was an easy voyage on to
Queenstown, where Irish emigrants embarked. Of course,
the new Trafalgar dry dock, completed in 1905, was a
special enticement for shipping companies.

Although White Star retained its main office in
Liverpool, its operational centre effectively moved to
Southampton; and where White Star went, Harland &
Wolff followed, with ancillary maintenance and outfitters'
workshops. Unemployment, a problem in Southampton in

the early years of the twentieth century, disappeared. The town boomed.

But it wasn't all plain sailing. London & South-Western Railway (LSWR), which had poured money into the town and renovated the South-Western Hotel in 1882, was quite happy to invest heavily in the 'new' port, and White Star was able and willing to provide employment opportunities for crews, just as Harland & Wolff could hire construction workers. But the companies needed longer quays and deeper docks, as well as larger and deeper channels for the massive new liners. They also needed wide expanses of water for the tugs to swing the ships around.

The River Itchen and the quays were controlled by the Harbour Board, and when White Star's local manager, Philip Curry, wrote to its members in December 1908, he had no reason to expect any objection to his request for improvements to facilities.

It is with pleasure that we have to inform you that with the object of bringing their Southampton–New York service up to the highest standard of efficiency, and of developing to the fullest extent the traffic via Southampton, the management of the Oceanic Steam Navigation Company Limited (White Star Line) are now having built at Messrs Harland & Wolff's shipbuilding yards at Belfast two steamships of the highest class, which will provide every attraction and comfort for travellers . . . and which will much exceed in tonnage any vessels now afloat or under construction. It will be obvious to your Board that if the

Port of Southampton is to derive full benefit from the advent of these steamers, it must be safeguarded against any possibility of reproach, or reflection upon its facilities, such as would arise were detention to be caused to the vessels in consequence of any deficiency in the draught of water in the channels to the port and docks.

We therefore deem it our duty to inform you that the builders estimate that these two vessels, when ready for sea in the Southampton service, will draw approximately 35 feet of water, and it is to be expected that on their arrival at this port from New York their draught will be in the neighbourhood of 32 feet 6 inches (less coal, fewer passengers by the end of the trip). The steamers may be expected to take up their places in the service in the spring of 1912 [of course *Olympic* was in service considerably earlier] and we confidently hope to receive an assurance from your Board that whatever dredging may be necessary to enable them to sail promptly, and to land their passengers without detention will be undertaken and completed before they are delivered.

The letter does sound a little threatening, and it is clear that White Star didn't want to foot the bill for any structural improvements that were going to be of some importance. But although Southampton wanted the money White Star would bring in, they were chary about the degree of investment they were expected to make. In February 1909 the Harbour Board's commissioner, Mr A. J. Day, commented, with a good deal of caution and foot-dragging: 'It does not seem necessary at the present time to do more than acknowledge this letter and state [that] when the proper time arrives it will receive the serious consideration of the committee ... As Mr Curry states in his letter that these new steamers ... will not be coming to Southampton before the spring of 1912, there can be no great urgency in dealing with this most important question of further dredging ...'

Nothing happened for almost a year, but in January 1910 a White Star deputation of big guns confronted the Harbour Board. It was led by Harold Sanderson, White Star's general manager and a close friend of Bruce Ismay. Backing him up were Philip Curry, White Star's marine superintendent in Southampton, Benjamin Steele, Herbert Haddock, and Southampton's chief pilot, George Bowyer. The Harbour Board Committee pointed out that it hesitated 'to incur such a heavy expense – some £100,000 – for the benefit of two vessels which may or may not require more water than the 32 feet we have now ... without securing a return to pay the interest to the stockholders and provide for the sinking fund'. Sanderson, on behalf of White Star, naturally retaliated by pointing out, not unreasonably, that the outlay on the work would be more than repaid by the income it would generate: 'These large ships pay large sums of money in wages and it is not very hard to my mind to see that Southampton derives some benefit in the large sums of money directly or indirectly brought to the town by the crews and their dependants and the men who work the ships in port. I do not think it is fair that we should be looked harshly at for being the first people to bring large ships to Southampton. We were not the first to produce large ships, and we shall be followed in a short time by others.'

Nevertheless, the row continued until finally LSWR stumped up the cash, though the Harbour Board's committee was replaced with a less blinkered group of people. In fact, further dredging proved necessary following *Titanic*'s near collision with the *City of New York*, a much smaller vessel whose moorings were broken by the suction power of *Titanic*'s massive hull as she was manoeuvred out of port for the short crossing to Cherbourg on the first leg of her maiden voyage.

PROGRESS AND DEVELOPMENT

White Star and Harland & Wolff had no such problems with the Belfast Harbour Commissioners. Neither did they with those of New York, where, so great was J. P. Morgan's influence, the White Star quays were extended (at tax-payers' expense) by 100 feet to accommodate the new giant liners. In Belfast, as the *Belfast News Letter* reported on 21 October 1910, work commenced on a new graving or dry dock in 1903, which was completed in time for *Olympic*'s occupancy in 1911: 'Belfast now has the honour of having built the largest ship ever launched [*Oceanic*, 1899], and it will soon have the distinction of being in possession of the biggest graving dock ever constructed. The work in connection with this necessary adjunct to modern and successful shipbuilding enterprise is now in its final stages, and it is expected that the dock will be ready for the admission of vessels in December, or in January at the very latest, but the formal opening will not take place until the summer.' Named the Thompson Graving Dock, in honour of the chairman of the Harbour Commissioners of the day, it was 850 feet long – extendable by a further 37½ feet – and carried 332 cast-iron keel-blocks to bear the weight of the huge ships it was designed to accommodate. It cost something approaching £350,000 – a huge sum a century ago.

In the meantime, the new Slips 2 and 3 were crowned with an enormous gantry, constructed by the Scottish engineering firm of Sir William Arrol & Company, responsible among other things for the Forth Bridge.

The gantry covered a massive area – 840 × 270 feet, and 228 feet high at its tallest point. It was made up of three rows of eleven towers, each row 121 feet from the next, and each tower weighing more than 6,000 tons. It accommodated a number of cranes, but in addition, in order to lift heavy machinery such as the engines, a 200-ton floating crane made by Benrather Engineering of Düsseldorf, Germany, at a cost of £30,000, was installed at the fitting-out berth for the new liners. It stood 150 feet high and its two hooks could lift up to 200 tons between them.

With these enormously significant improvements, Belfast's position as the world's leading shipyard was confirmed, and the city basked in a sense of civic pride and international importance. The *Belfast News Letter* reported in glowing terms on 21 October 1910: 'It is a matter of real gratification to all of us in Belfast that the *Olympic* and the *Titanic* should be built here, and in undertaking the construction of vessels of such enormous proportions, it is felt that Messrs. Harland & Wolff are maintaining their own splendid traditions and at the same time indicating the right of the Ulster capital to be reckoned as one of the great shipbuilding centres in the world.'

CHAPTER FOUR

NUMBER 401

DETAILED PLANS FOR *TITANIC* were first drawn up in the large, barrel-roofed drawing office of Harland & Wolff. Models were built, and later much larger drawings were made on the floor of the mould loft, a huge, multi-windowed space where the loftsmen used massive pencils – 18 inches long and 1¼ inches in diameter – to mark out the cross-section of the ship at full size, and the length at

---

'There were hardly any women working in shipbuilding at the time. The only jobs done by women during the construction of *Titanic* were in the drawing rooms. In the days before photocopiers, everything was drawn by hand, and the original plans had to be seen by many people, so women were employed to copy and trace plans that would be distributed throughout the shipyard.'

one-quarter scale. This was the beginning of a long, arduous and extremely complex process, which is described in the following pages.

THE LOGISTICS OF BUILDING A LINER

Construction of a large liner began with the ordering of its components, and those for *Olympic* and *Titanic* were ordered mostly at the same time. The list was long, supplied where possible in order of installation, and included:

- flat-plate keel
- stem
- stern
- bottom plating
- floors
- keelsons and tank top
- side framing and plating
- bulkheads
- girders and pillars
- decks
- struts
- hatches
- manhole doors
- sidelights (portholes)
- rudder
- masts and rigging
- steering gear
- ballast
- plumbing
- heating and electrical systems
- ventilation and refrigeration plants
- lifeboats
- furniture and other stateroom and public-room appointments

This list is not comprehensive: it is designed to give just an idea of the myriad parts required. Simply compiling it was a massive responsibility. Then there was the ordering to be done, bearing in mind the logistics of transporting precision-made heavy castings from places outside Belfast and ensuring their safe and punctual delivery. (It took twenty shire horses, operated by the haulage company W. A. Rees, to pull *Titanic's* central anchor from Noah Hingley's works in Dudley to the station, whence it was transported by special train on the London & North-Western Railway to Fleetwood, and from there shipped to Belfast on the F. W. Kemp steamer *Duke of Albany*.) On the whole, if material arrived ahead of its place in the schedule while items that should have preceded it weren't yet in, work started immediately on that material, and the finished product was set aside until the proper time came for it to be installed.

WORK IN PROGRESS

The Olympic-class ships were designed to conform with Board of Trade regulations governing passenger and emigrant ships. *Olympic* and *Titanic* had eight passenger decks. From top to bottom these were the Boat deck, Promenade deck (Deck A), Bridge deck (B), Shelter deck (C), Saloon deck (D), Upper deck (E), Middle deck (F) and Lower deck (G). At each end of the ship was an Orlop deck, and just above keel level was the Tank top, which defined the double-bottom, and supported the engines and other machinery.

Work on the laying of *Titanic's* keel began on 31 March 1909, and it then took twenty-six months of building the hull until it was ready to be launched. The

LOGGING DELIVERIES

Directors' minute-books logged the materials bought in to build the Olympic-class ships. A sample of these laboriously handwritten pages includes:

1908
James Miller & Co: 1,000 tons rivets
Wm. Oliver & Son: 700 pieces varnished oak
D. Colville & Sons: 3,000 tons steel angles and channels
D. Colville & Sons: 2,000 tons steel boiler plates
H. Hutton & Co: 285 logs pitch pine

1911
Gregory Lawson & Co: 10 tons 2 inch ingots (£192 to £195 per ton)
W. L. Laycock & Co: 10 tons hair (7d. to 2/- per lb)
Harrison Robinson & Co: 60 logs Oregon pine (1/11 per cubic foot)
Thomas Edwards & Son: Cargo Tobasco mahogany (£10 per ton)
Wm. Jacks & Co: 400 tons No. 3 Eglinton pig iron (56/10 per ton)
Cookson & Co: 20 tons dry red lead (£15. 7/6)

ship was built at a time of great innovation and incorporated many new elements within a traditional design. Essentially, with the keel acting as a kind of backbone, the structure was a massive box constructed of girders forming ribs. The hull was then covered with steel shell plating, which in *Titanic*'s case was arranged clinker-fashion (overlapping) from the keel to the turn of the bilge, and from that point upwards was laid using the 'in-and-out' system (like stitching). The entire structure was held together by rivets of various design – 3 million of them – with an aggregate weight of 1,200 tons, and this doesn't include those used to manufacture the boilers and other machinery that powered the ship. The rivets were fitted either by machine (the steel rivets were fitted amidships by machine riveters) or by hand.

Riveters were skilled workers, whether operating hydraulic machinery or hand-working in teams with riveting hammers. Theirs was a dangerous and desperately noisy job, though in fact the construction of *Titanic* resulted in only eight fatalities overall – and this was with a safety standard of one death per £100,000 spent. There were no hard hats in those days, no heat-resistant overalls, no protective goggles. All you had was your common sense, your experience and the watchful eyes of your workmates.

For the most part, riveters' worst professional risks were deafness and, through general stress and physical wear and tear, a life expectancy of about sixty years. They were also paid piecework, not by the hour, which some critics now consider ill advised. Such a policy, they argue, would have encouraged workers to skimp. But they didn't do this because, apart from anything else, they were supervised by rivet-counters, a job that must have been almost mind-bogglingly tedious.

A riveting team of hand-riveters consisted of three men and a boy assistant. Two of the men worked on the outside of the hull, each armed with a heavy hammer. Within the hull was the 'holder-up', or third man. His job, for which he wielded an even heavier hammer, was to hold the rivet in place with his hammer while its hot outer point was hammered flat. The boy attended the man on the inside, and his job was to heat the rivets until red-hot in a portable furnace. Then, with the aid of pincers, he transferred the hot rivets to the holes already bored in the frame and plate. The outer men hit the point of the rivet with quick alternating blows, so the noise they endured was continuous, and the number of riveters was legion.

The overall engineering design criteria were high and hard to achieve, since a luxury passenger ship not only has to be a sort of floating hotel that delivers relative stability on seas that can be rough, but also has to withstand the huge stresses and strains imposed by such seas. Hull construction was well described in a lecture given to the Belfast Natural History and Philosophical Society by Alec Wilson on Friday, 5 November 1915:

The keel is laid upon the top of the keel blocks placed to receive it . . . Upon the keel the keel-plate is erected, which forms a sort of spinal column for the future vessel. The lower part, or tank, is then proceeded with and after its completion . . . the rib framing is begun . . . When the framing approaches completion the deckbeams are begun . . . the ship is of course one immense steel girder, and its strength depends largely upon the design and construction of the sub-girders . . . When the framing is completed the plating is begun, and the hydraulic riveters are concentrated upon those portions where there are special stresses, principally along the bilges and sheer strakes. (These latter being the uppermost 'planks' in a hull's plating.) The plates are commonly doubled at these parts, the thickness of the steel skin thus being about 2.25 inches and the diameter of the rivets 1.125 inches . . . the plates used for the sheer strake, the upper part of the skin of the ship, run up to about 36 feet long, 6 feet 6 inches broad, by 1.125 inches thick, and weigh over 4 tons.

No wonder so much heavy construction equipment was necessary! And, as the specialist magazine *Shipbuilder* reported in 1911, 'Some idea of the great importance of the riveting in the *Olympic* and the *Titanic* will be gathered from the fact that there are half-a-million rivets in the double-bottom of each vessel, weighing about 270 tons . . .' And here the rivets were an impressive 1¼ inches in diameter.

Riveting was also very skilled and precise work, for the entire strength of the ship depended on it. There was a lack of skilled riveters, and their work, given a workforce of about 4,500, which was nearly a third of all Harland & Wolff employees at the time, was not always easy to supervise. It is interesting to reflect that Number 3 ('best') iron rivets were used rather than Number 4 ('best best'). Number 3s contained a higher slag content than 4s, and the latter were used in most other ships at the time. However, the use of Number 3s didn't necessarily contribute directly to the disaster, for where the iceberg buckled (not gashed, as was once thought) the plates, allowing sea water in between them, the stronger steel rivets, driven home by hydraulic riveting machines, had been used. And it's worth bearing in mind too that Olympic, built to similar specifications, gave twenty-four years of more or less blameless service. But even so, it is good to remember these circumstances, especially in the wake of the inquiries that followed the sinking, and Shan Bullock's flowery comments in his uncritical biography of Thomas Andrews, written soon after Andrews' undoubtedly heroic death: 'Good enough in the shipyard is never enough. Think what scamped [sic] work, a flawed shaft, a badly laid plate, an error in calculation, may mean some wild night out in the Atlantic; and when you are next in Belfast go to Queen's Island, and see there, in the shops, on the slips, how everyone is striving, or being made to strive, on your behalf and that of all who voyage, for the absolute best – everything to a hair's breadth, all as strong and sound as hands can achieve.'

Overall, though, riveting remained at the core of a ship's structure, and skimping would never be in the interest of owners or builders as resultant repairs would be costly to effect and also keep the ship out of service. Even so, partial or extensive replating works were not uncommon, since riveting depended on a very precise alignment of the holes in the plates through which the rivets were passed, a difficult thing to do when workers were dealing with hundreds of feet of straking, and with about thirty different kinds of rivet, depending on where the work was being done. The rivets, depending on type, had to be heated up to different degrees as well, so there was much to consider. Hydraulic riveting was more predictably accurate than hand riveting, but the machines couldn't always be positioned where man could get to, and iron rivets were more malleable than steel, and hence were used where manual teams were employed.

KEEL

The vertical keel plate, or central keelson, was 4 feet 4 inches wide at its widest point. It was held together with hydraulically driven rivets, which also connected it to the keel plate and keel bar below it. These in turn rested on specially designed and scrupulously aligned wooden keel blocks, all laid at the right angle of inclination to ensure a smooth launch a couple of years later. From this basic foundation structure, *Titanic*'s bottom began to take shape. This was a double-bottom, built on a system of rectangular cells to guarantee maximum strength, especially under that part of the hull where the massive reciprocating engines would be placed. Here its depth was increased from a little over 5 feet to just over 6 feet. Within the double-bottom, a structure of extreme rigidity, the water-ballast tanks would be installed, the girders used having holes in them to make them lighter except where ballast-tanks were to be separated. Once completed, the Tank top forming the upper floor of the double-bottom was plated in fore-and-aft strakes, and timber shores were already in place to support the now easily recognizable lowest part of the hull.

Manholes were let into the plating to allow maintenance access to the ballast-tanks, which were designed to hold 5,754 tons of fresh water and boiler feed-water.

SKELETON

Once the keel and the Tank top were finished, the next stage of construction concerned the frames, or transverse ribs, which were of various designs and sizes depending on where they were to be used. These, supported by girders, pillars and beams, made up the skeleton of the ship. This gigantic scaffolding was spaced out with frames relatively close to one another. For this purpose, the hull had to be divided into a series of numbered fore and aft (F and A) segments from an unnumbered central point in the precise middle of the ship. The frames either side of this central position were designated 1F and 1A, and so on fore and aft until reaching the aftermost frame, 148A, and the foremost, 156F. Fore numbers 156–134 were spaced at 2 feet; 134–119 at 2 feet 3 inches; 119–107 at 2 feet 6 inches; 107–95 at 2 feet 9 inches; and 95 to amidships at 3 feet. Moving aft, amidships to 111 were at 3 feet; 111–121 at 2 feet 9 inches; 121–133 at 2 feet 6 inches; 133–148 at 2 feet 3 inches.

Erecting the structure was exacting. Girders were cut to slightly longer than required. The rivet holes were punched in and then the girders were bent to shape before being trimmed to their exact size. The rest of the structure was made up principally of web-frames for greater strength and rigidity, beams to unite the frames in terms of struts

'Men worked with their brothers, their fathers, uncles, neighbours and friends.' Harland & Wolff workers leaving the shipyard in May 1911.

The main players. Financier John Pierpont Morgan (*above*) on board his yacht, *Corsair III*, and *Titanic*'s principal designer, Thomas Andrews (*below left*), pictured here in his crumpled working suit in 1911. Andrews' uncle and Harland & Wolff chairman, Lord Pirrie, makes a tour of inspection of the ship just before her launch with the head of White Star Line, J. Bruce Ismay (*below right*).

'The biggest and most spectacular boat in the world.' A poster advertises the newly completed *Titanic* ahead of her launch.

Detailed plans for *Titanic* were first drawn up in the large, barrel-roofed drawing office of Harland & Wolff (*above*); it was the beginning of a long, arduous and extremely complex process. Later, workers fitted the blades to the turbine rotor (*below*) and operated seven-ton hydraulic riveting machines (*right*, on *Titanic*'s sister ship *Britannic*).

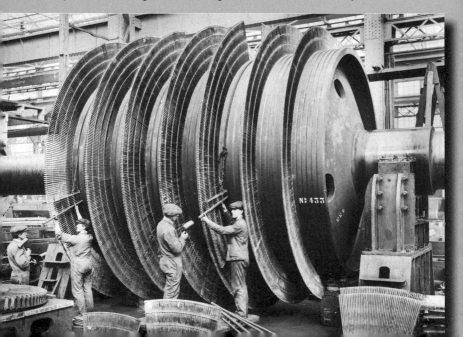

N° 433

One of *Titanic*'s anchors, cast in Dudley and weighing more than 16 tons, is carted to the train for transport to Liverpool and thence Belfast (*above left*). The men's size gives a sense of the immense scale of *Titanic* and her sister liners as the workers fit the starboard tail shaft to the stern of Titanic (*below left*) and *Olympic*'s number 4 funnel is wheeled out of the workshops for installation (*below*).

The port side of the stem of *Olympic* in the biggest graving dock ever constructed, the Thompson Graving Dock, Belfast. The chimney of the pump-house is visible in the background.

and ties and to support the deck-plating, and solid, vertical pillars that supported the transverse beams. Extra support was given to the engine- and boiler-room floors.

The near-vertical stem, which is the foremost part of the hull, was formed from castings and bars made by the Darlington Forge Company and totalled 7.5 tons in weight. It was joined to the keel by a cast-steel forefoot weighing an additional 3.5 tons, and was a virtual upward extension of the keel, bound securely to the main structure by the shell plating.

At the other end of the ship, the stern frame was designed to provide support for the rudder and the shaft for the centre propeller, which would be driven by *Titanic*'s turbine engine. It had a hole in it, of course, through which the shaft connected to the propeller. There was a stern-post to which the rudder was attached, and this also supported the somewhat slender but still massive rudder. The post needed to be as strongly built as possible because the lower part of it stood free of the hull itself, and it had to withstand the vibrations set up by the propeller and the lateral force exerted by the rudder as it turned.

The whole assembly, and the brackets that would support the port and starboard propellers, driven by the two reciprocating engines, was designed by Harland & Wolff, as was the rudder itself. But each of the huge constituent parts was made by the Darlington Forge Company, and nearly all the pieces were manufactured from Siemens-Martin mild steel. The rudder gudgeons – the lugs forged on the stern-post on which the rudder was hung and hinged – were lined with removable gunmetal bushings since these holes took a lot of strain, and replacing worn-out bushings was easier, faster and less costly than replacing the whole post.

Similarly, the stern frame itself was cast in two pieces, bound together by scarves (joints made by notching the ends of two pieces of timber or metal so that they lock together end to end). The justification for this was that if one part (usually the lower) were damaged, it could be replaced without the need for replacing the whole stern-post. This plan failed, though, when *Olympic* collided much later with the *Fort St George* in New York harbour and the resultant damage was so severe that the entire stern frame of *Olympic* had to be replaced. Some indication of the difficulty of doing this may be deduced from the fact that the frame weighed 70 tons and had a height of just over 67 feet.

The two wing propeller bracket casts stood clear of the line of the hull, but were cased in steel plates called bossings.

RUDDER

The rudder was of a type called 'unbalanced', meaning that all its effective turning area was aft of the rudder stock. Although this allowed less manoeuvrability and demanded a more powerful steering engine, the design of the stern and the position of the propellers on the Olympic-class ships made this design a requirement. *Titanic*'s rudder was made in six pieces: the stock, of forged steel, 23½ inches in diameter, and five plates of mild steel – the rudder proper – bolted together with the boltheads at the top so that the bolts would stay in place in the unlikely event of the nut working loose. To make sure this wouldn't happen, the bolt-heads and the nuts, once firmly secured, were covered in Portland cement, which was streamlined into the ribs of the adjacent section. The additional effect of the cement was to reduce both corrosion and turbulence. The completed rudder was attached to the gudgeons on the stern-post by means of seven pintles, which distributed the weight of the 101.25-ton rudder between them and were secured by nuts. The rudder itself was nearly 79 feet long and 15¼ feet wide at its widest point.

AN UNSINKABLE SHIP?

Much has been made of the claim that *Titanic* was unsink-able. In fact, no one connected with her, or any serious publication, ever made such a claim. The word was seized out of context by the press in the wake of the disaster following a nervous remark by White Star vice-president Philip A. S. Franklin, reported in the *New York Times* on 16 April 1912: 'I thought her unsinkable and I based my opinion on the best expert advice available. I do not under-stand it.' The most *Titanic*'s builders and designers claimed was that she was *virtually* or *practically* unsinkable. However, they must have believed in that declaration. Their belief was based on the succession of watertight bulkheads constructed at intervals throughout her length: these were pierced by watertight doors that allowed access between them in normal use, but could be closed fast in the event of an accident. Once the doors were closed, the bulkheads were sealed, and *Titanic* was designed in such a way that she would not sink if any four of her forward watertight compartments were flooded – and it was the forward compartments that were most likely to bear the brunt of any accident.

In the event, as we know, *Titanic* was sufficiently damaged for the pumps to be unable to keep pace with the inrush of water, since more than four compartments had been breached. The liner was in fact breached along 300 feet of her starboard side, and the five forward compartments were flooded to a depth of 14 feet above the keel within ten minutes. The ship was doomed. Later it was argued that she might still have survived if the watertight bulkheads had been extended higher than the deck level they actually reached, and this improvement, along with many others, was made to both sister ships in the wake of the accident.

White Star publicity from 1911 boasted: 'There are fifteen transverse watertight bulkheads, extending from the double-bottom to the upper deck at the forward end of the ship and to the saloon deck at the after end – in both instances far above the waterline . . . The watertight doors in a vessel of this size are, of course, a most important item . . . They are of Harland & Wolff's special design, of massive construction, and provided with oil cataracts [*sic*] governing the closing speed.' The bulkheads lettered (from forward) A to P, omitting the letter I (which could be mistaken for the numeral 1), were distributed pretty evenly throughout the length of the ship. They were raised to either E or D decks, depending on their position, but well above the waterline and, as with the lifeboats, well above the minimum Board of Trade safety requirements. There was no real reason to expect an accident of such proportions, and much of *Titanic's* legendary status depends on the extraordinary concatenation of circumstances that led to the tragedy. The truths behind the accident were a little tougher, but whatever the case, the lessons learnt were learnt the hard way.

The first bulkhead, A, was called the collision bulkhead, and set about 44 feet from the bow since it had itself to be protected from serious damage to the stem, and the distance was not great enough to allow any inrush of water to have a serious effect on the vessel's integrity. The aftermost bulkhead, P, was positioned just behind the propellers and was designed to counter any inrush of water caused by a broken shaft. Bulkheads E to J were placed halfway between the coal-bunkers, which were located fore and aft of each boiler-room, and these were special in that their watertight doors were placed at the ends of watertight tunnels running aft between 9 and 13½ feet through the bunkers themselves. The bulkheads had the additional advantage of adding to the strength of the liner's construction, and they were fitted to the inner shell plating by angle-bars, tightly fitted and caulked.

The watertight doors that, when raised, provided the necessary access through the bulkheads rose and fell in a vertical plane and differed in size depending on where they were placed. Bulkheads D to J had doors that were 5½ feet high and 4 feet wide, since these ran through the boiler-rooms and needed to accommodate the passage of large numbers of men, as well as coal-carrying wheelbarrows. The doors connecting the bulkheads from K onwards aft were narrower, at 5½ feet high by 2¾ feet wide. Each door ran in a groove, and the edges were fitted on each side with six wedges, cast as part of the door, that fitted as the door was lowered into corresponding 'receiving' wedge-shaped lugs on the door-frame. These wedges and receivers were very carefully machined and lapped so that, when pressed together, they created the watertightness desired. The doors were designed to close relatively slowly, except for the last 18–24 inches, depending on the door's size. This was to allow escaping crew the maximum opportunity to get on the safe side of whichever door they were passing through, but the guillotine effect of the last couple of feet meant that the heavy door (the heaviest weighed around 15 cwt) would cut through or cast aside any object preventing it from falling fully into place and thus attaining full water-tightness. The doors were operated by remote control from the bridge, which released all the doors simultaneously.

After the demise of *Titanic*, *Olympic* was fitted with a remote control capable of closing doors independently, but on *Titanic* there was at least a local override by each door and on the deck immediately above it. A system of bells operated from the bridge warned of the imminent closure of the doors, which took about thirty seconds to close before the final drop. 'A ladder or escape is provided in each boiler-room, engine room and similar watertight compartment, in order that the closing of the doors at any time shall not imprison the men working therein; though the risk of this eventuality is lessened by electric bells placed in the vicinity of each door, which ring prior to their closing, and thus give warning to those below,' asserted White Star publicity.

In addition, lateral-sliding watertight doors were installed on D and E decks where the bulkheads impinged on passenger-occupied territory. This worked on a similar principle, and although they could not have the final snap shut of the vertical doors, they were cranked closed and anything caught in them – a far less likely event on passenger decks – could be removed. The doors were painted to fit in with the surrounding decor – either in white, for example, or wood-grain effect. And there were also some hinged watertight doors, closed (as often seen in shipwreck movies) by a series of handles that compressed a rubber seal between the edge of the door and a receiving lip on the door-frame.

'Then into shop after shop in endless succession, each needing a day's journey to traverse, each wonderfully clean and ordered, and all full of a wonders: boilers as tall as houses, shafts a boy's height in diameter, enormous propellers . . . turbine motors on which workmen clambered as upon a cliff, huge lathes, pneumatic hammers, and quiet slow-moving machines that dealt with cold steel, shearing it, punching it, planing it, as if it had been so much dinner cheese. Then up into the Moulding Loft, large enough for a football ground, and its floor a beautiful maze of frame lines; on through the Joiners' shops, with their tools that can do everything but speak; through the Smiths' shops, with their long rows of helmet-capped hearths, on into the great airy building . . . where an army of Cabinetmakers are fashioning all kinds of ship's furniture. Then across into the Central power station, daily generating enough electricity to light Belfast. On into the fine arched Drawing Hall where the spirit of Tom Andrews seemed still to linger, and into his office where often he sat drafting those reports, so exhaustively minute, so methodical and neatly penned, which now have such pathetic and revealing interest.'

Shan Bullock, *Thomas Andrews, Shipbuilder*, 1912

PLATING AND SHEATHING

The ship was sheathed and decked in steel plating, which added to the solidity of her structure. The steel used was mild (low-carbon) steel of high-grade 'battleship' quality that had to be rolled out by machines. As an anonymous technician recalled: 'You fed your heated steel plate from the furnace into the machine, where you could bend and curve it as required. The biggest plates on the ship were 30 feet long and weighed more than three tons each. The rolling machines were dangerous beasts. As one pushed the steel plates into them, it was all too easy to get one's fingers, hands and arms dragged in too. There was no emergency stop button, and if one got caught there'd be nothing to stop one being dragged in bodily and crushed to death.'

The strakes (horizontal steel plates) on *Titanic* were numbered from A, first out from the keel bar, up to Z at the level of the Bridge deck. The joints between the inner and outer strakes of the steel plating were filled with liners of iron or steel. The entire system was both intricate and demanding, calling as it did for the highest precision on a very large scale. The average shell plate on *Titanic* amidships was 6 feet wide, 1 inch thick (though tapering at each end) and 30 feet long, adding up to a weight of 4.25 tons. Lower down, on the bottom of the ship, thicker plates were used, and various other parts of the ship required specialized plating. Keels in the shape of projecting fins were fitted along the bilge (the rounded part of the hull where the bottom joins the sides) for about 295 feet of *Titanic*'s length amidships to act as stabilizers.

In addition to all the work described above, expansion joints had to be allowed for. Two were fitted on *Titanic* – one at frame 49F and the other at 28A. All joints had to be caulked after the parts had been riveted together. This was done in the case of the Olympic-class and other large liners by using a variety of special blunt-ended chisels to nip the prepared edges of the joints tightly together, a process known as faying. This was vital to ensure absolute water-tightness. And finally, the various openings in the steel hull – coal-ports, access doors, sidelight openings and so on – were made, and the doors and portholes fitted and made watertight.

DECKING AND CAULKING

Decking was also carefully laid since it had to have a camber to ensure water fall-off to the scuppers, which drained it overboard. The camber was not pronounced, but again the work required a high degree of precision. The steel decking was laid and then holes were cut into it for engine and boiler casings, hatches, companionways and so on, and the surrounds of these strengthened by putting thicker or doubled-up deck plating in their vicinity. Caulking was applied to joints and the steel was coated with a bitumen product to prevent water seepage through the decks, which would cause havoc if, for example, it got into the dynamo room. Finally, the wooden deck planking was cut and laid above all living spaces, though some areas were left clear until after engines and boilers had been shipped and installed to obviate damage. The resulting insulation, though necessary and very effective, created another water problem – that of condensation. To counter this, all exposed metal ceilings were coated with a preparation of granulated cork before being painted with at least three coats of paint.

The wood used for *Titanic*'s exposed decking was best-quality yellow pine, and the planking was attached using galvanized iron nuts and bolts. The ends of the bolts were countersunk and covered with matching wooden plugs to conceal them, and the gaps between the planks were filled first with a layer of cotton, then of oakum, then pitch. After that the decking was planed (using a recently invented electric machine) and varnished. Portions of the deck subject to especially hard wear were laid with pitch pine, and teak was used for all the planking where the decks met the sides of the hull, and for the surrounds of all waterways, hatches, scuttles, deckhouses, windlasses, cranes, ventilators and other deck fitments and machinery. Interior decking was also wood, though bathrooms, lavatories, pantries and galleys were floored in tile or brick.

STEELWORK

By the time of her launch, *Titanic*'s steelwork was more or less complete, as was a good deal of her superstructure. Funnels, boilers, engines, propellers and upper superstructure would be fitted after the launch, in the fitting-out wharf, though for the purposes of this book, some of these elements are dealt with in this pre-launch section. While the work on *Titanic* seems enormous, it's worth remembering that in 1911 Harland & Wolff launched nine other ships. The total tonnage amounted to 118,209, and total horsepower to 97,000. It was the greatest output of any shipyard in any one year in history.

Harland & Wolff was doing well financially too. Profits were up to £110,000, and the workforce had expanded from just under 11,400 in 1910 to almost 15,000 in 1911.

At the same time, expansion and improvement of the ship-yard itself was planned to take place over the next couple of years, at a cost of £250,000. The optimism this represented was backed by a bulging order book. The periodical *Syren & Shipping* reported on the positive mood in June 1911: 'There is, moreover, every reason to anticipate that the firm's output of tonnage during the current year will beat all records. It need scarcely be remarked that an establishment with a production capacity such as is indicated . . . is . . . one of the best laid-out and most perfectly equipped yards in the world . . . No visitor going over the establishment can fail to be impressed with the well-ordered activity which prevails everywhere . . . the spirit of modernity or of a mature youthfulness suffuses everything.'

ENGINES AND DECKHOUSES

While the construction of the hull was going on, the machinery shops had built and tested the engines, then partially taken them apart again for transport to the fitting-out deepwater wharf. Other fitments concurrently under construction – boilers, machinery, funnels and so on – were now transported to the wharf to be hoisted aboard by the floating crane, and settled in the places appointed for them. Once these major works had been completed, the decking could be finished off, the six cargo hatches supplied with coamings and covers, bulwarks, railings and awnings fitted, and the superstructure completed.

The Boat decks, designated A and B, were deckhouse structures. Most of these were made of steel, but some were wooden, and most were prefabricated alongside the building of the hull and installed in the fitting-out wharf after *Titanic*'s launch. The wooden structures were the wheelhouse and the navigating bridge because steel would have affected the accuracy of the ship's compasses. For the same reason, all metal fittings within 10 feet of the compasses were made of bronze or brass. The wood used was principally teak for all parts directly exposed to the weather, and the structures were made in the joiners' shop, put together for testing, then broken up into component parts for reassembly during the fitting-out.

Both the wheelhouse and the navigating bridge were fitted with large, sturdily built windows for maximum visibility. Sidelights or portholes were also sturdily built, with various safety features. In heavy weather a disc of heavy steel could be placed over the glass. Similar plugs could be mounted externally, and these were used routinely at night for all portholes forward of the bridge because any light would affect the night vision of the officers on watch. Special 'self-ventilating' sidelights were used in the crew's quarters, in lavatories and everywhere close to the waterline. These allowed the admission of air, but a built-in mechanism would automatically make them watertight should the need arise. The specialized portholes and windows on *Titanic* were made by Thomas Utley & Company of Liverpool, a firm still in operation and in the same family today.

Utley was offered a complimentary ticket for the maiden voyage, but turned down the invitation to sail, following a premonition of his wife's. How he reacted to the news of the wreck, in which he would almost certainly have perished, is not recorded. His grandson was recently asked to verify that a sidelight allegedly recovered from the wreck was authentic. On checking its serial number against the company records, he found that it was, and, even after almost a hundred years in the depths of the Atlantic, it took only two days' restoration to bring it back to near-mint condition.

Windows proper, installed in public rooms such as the first-class lounge and the reading and writing room, were teak-framed and built by Utley's to various bespoke patterns. Internal windows in first class had heavily etched decoration, and leaded and stained glass were also used in accordance with the neo-Gothic taste of the period.

MASTS AND FUNNELS

Titanic had two masts placed about 600 feet from each other, and made of steel, except for a top section of 15 feet that was made from teak. The masts, about 3 feet in diameter near the bottom, rose about 155 feet above deck level and were intended to support rigging and derricks for loading cargo, and to carry the Marconi wireless aerial. They slanted gently aft in the same plane as the funnels, and were supported by a system of steel stays and shrouds. The foremast carried the crow's nest, a sheet-steel basket equipped with a portable telephone and a large alarm bell, and it was reached by means of a ladder within the mast. The after mast, or mainmast, was marginally shorter, and the Marconi aerial was slung between the two.

The great defining feature of *Titanic* and her sisters, as well as the big contemporary Cunarders, was their four elegant funnels, which gave a sense of the ships' power and speed and attracted admiring crowds. The *Northern Whig* newspaper reported on 10 November 1911: 'Many hundreds of visitors to Belfast during the last few weeks have taken a tram-car ride down to the end of the Queen's Road . . . and there lay the *Titanic*, with her stupendous deck erections still in the rough and only a dozen or two of artisans flitting like ants about her decks . . .'

The first three funnels took up the smoke and hot gases from the boiler furnaces. They were double-walled, the inner funnel being the actual flue. The size of each inner funnel depended on the fire-grate area it serviced, which differed from funnel to funnel. Rain-guards were positioned at two places along the height of each. The aftermost fourth funnel was part of the ship's ventilation system. It channelled away stale air from the galleys on D deck, the B deck first-class A La Carte Restaurant, the pantries, the first-class smoking room and its fireplace (the only real coal-burning fireplace on the ship), the hospital facilities, various lavatories, and the turbine engine room.

The funnels were elliptical in cross-section, measuring about 24 × 19 feet, and they rose about 72 feet above the boat deck. Ladders ran up the forward sides of each to provide maintenance access to the ship's whistles, and each funnel was supported by twelve shrouds. As with the rest of the heavy equipment, the funnels were prefabricated and mounted in the fitting-out wharf.

Apart from the exterior painting of the hull and the fitting of the propellers, which would have to wait until the last stages of construction in dry dock, a huge further task remained in the form of onboard paintwork, final water-proofing and anti-corrosion work. Paint itself acted as an anti-corrosion agent, important in a vessel exposed to large amounts of salt water throughout its working life. Painters were included among the crew, and *Titanic* had a paint store on G deck. The paint used was thick, having a base of linseed oil. After years and many layers, paintwork built up to a very noticeable thickness, which might not have been very pleasing aesthetically, but it was very effective. Portland cement and varnishes were also used in the battle against corrosion, as well as proprietary brands such as Wailes, Dove & Company's Bitumastic. The latter was used in various forms in the boiler-rooms, lower passages and on the Tank top.

Where brass and bronze were set close to iron or steel (especially mild steel) and sea water was also present, they could have a severe corrosive effect. To counter this, protective slabs or strips of zinc known as 'sacrificial anodes' were placed on the hull near by. Although these too would be corroded, they could be replaced easily and their presence was very effective. The same technique, using special alloy anodes, is still used today on off-shore oil rigs. Soft iron was also effective, and cheaper and longer-lasting than zinc. Anti-fouling preparations, often rust-coloured, were applied annually to the parts of the hull in constant contact with water. Pipes and boilers were lagged with magnesia coverings manufactured by Newalls Insulation of Newcastle-upon-Tyne.

INJURIES

In the process of such a vast construction project, there were bound to be injuries and fatalities. Accidents that befell the workers often resulted in broken bones and crushed hands. Of the 246 injuries noted in *Titanic*'s injury log, twenty-eight are described as 'severe' – arms severed in machines, for example, and legs crushed by falling steel. Such injuries meant that those who sustained them would never work again. A memo of 10 April 1912 details the number of deaths and accidents, both 'severe' and 'slight', that occurred during the construction of *Titanic*. From it we learn that there were six deaths on the ship itself during construction and fitting out, and two further deaths in the works (that is, the workshops and sheds in the shipyard). The compensations paid out for these were respectively £795 5s 2d and £3,385 13s. Severe injuries totalled twenty-two – eighteen on board ship and four in the shipyard – with a total compensation of £2,101 16s 3d. There were ninety-nine slight injuries on board, and a further fifty-six in the yard, for which compensation of £664 14s 11d was paid. In the engine works there were no fatalities, but a total of six severe and sixty-three slight injuries.

The *Belfast News Letter* of 17 June 1911 reported one death, that of a forty-nine-year-old rivet counter called Robert Murphy, citing the testimony of an eye-witness: 'Witness saw the deceased put up his hand to count the rivets, and just with that the staging went down, and the deceased fell too. The ends of the deck gave way and fell to the staging below, the deceased dropping a distance of about 50 feet.'

The Murphys were a popular and well-established Protestant family. Robert senior, a member of the Orange Order, the Royal Black Preceptory (which promoted the Scripture and the principles of the Protestant Reformation) and the Rechabites (an alcohol abstention league), was also treasurer of the Boilermakers' Union and a member of the Select Vestry of the Church. The *Irish Daily Telegraph* carried the following report of his death on 17 June 1911:

KILLED ON TITANIC
Riveter's sad death – A singularly pathetic case

In the Old Recorder's Court, Belfast, the city coroner (Dr. James Graham) held an inquest touching the death of Robert James Murphy, 49, of 6 Hillman Street, Belfast, a rivet-counter, who was fatally injured on board the White Star liner *Titanic*, at present in course of construction at Messrs. Harland & Wolff on 13th inst., succumbing to his injuries the same evening in the Royal Victoria Hospital.

Mr. S. C. Porter (instructed by Mr. W. K. Gibson) appeared for the next-of-kin. Mr. Sydney Brant, H. M. Inspector of Factories, was in attendance, and the examination of witnesses was conducted by Head Constable Peate.

Mrs. Susannah Murphy, widow of the deceased, who was deeply affected, was examined. Her husband, she said, left home for his work on the morning of the accident at half-past five. She saw him in the Royal Victoria Hospital at half-past seven the same evening, but he was so ill that he was unable to speak to her. She had since identified the body.

William Blackmore, a riveter, deposed to having passed the deceased on a stage on the ship. Just as he stepped on to the ladder at the end he heard a thud, and the next thing he saw was the deceased lying in the hold. The staging in question comprised two planks.

Head-Constable Peate – How long was he on the staging?

Witness – Not more than a minute and a half.

Replying to further questions, witness said the planks had slipped and given way.

Mr. Brant asked if the planks had fallen away at the time of the accident, and the reply of the witness was in the affirmative.

When you left this staging was there any surging?

Witness – Nothing unusual.

Head-Constable Peate – Did you jump from the staging to the ladder?

Witness – No; I left it in the usual way.

What distance was it to the ladder?

Witness – It would not be more than eighteen inches, or two feet at the outside.

Mr. Porter – What do you think caused the planks to give?

Witness – I could not form any idea.

To a juror – One end of the staging rested on the deck and the other on a thwart.

Replying to further questions by Mr. Brant, witness said it was the end on the deck that gave way, the other remaining on the thwart.

Geo. Maginness, a paint boy in the employment of Messrs. Harland & Wolff, Ltd., described the accident. 'Deceased,' he said, 'walked along the staging, and the riveter [*sic*] walked by him. As he went by him the staging swung. I saw the deceased put up his hand to count the rivets, and just with that the staging went down, and deceased fell down too.' He added that the ends on the deck gave way and fell to the staging below, the deceased dropping a distance of about 50 feet.

Thomas Walsh, a riveter, stated that he had worked on that particular staging for two days. The planks were between four and six inches thick.

Dr. Anderson, of the Royal Victoria Hospital, described the deceased's injuries and expressed the opinion that death was due to shock following fracture of the skull.

Mr. Thomas Houston, yard manager for Messrs. Harland & Wolff, expressed his employers' regret at the tragic occurrence. The deceased, he said, was a most useful man and very careful. He was esteemed not only in Messrs. Harland & Wolff's, but also all over the city.

Mr. Porter said he appreciated very much Messrs.

Harland & Wolff's sympathy, adding that they always dealt very generously with their employees.

The Coroner said a fact that made that inquest a singularly pathetic one was that deceased's son had been killed about six months ago on the same ship. It was very gratifying to see Messrs. Harland & Wolff speaking so highly of the deceased, who, from what he had heard, had been held in high esteem.

The jury found in accordance with the medical evidence, adding that in their opinion the staging was not sufficient for the work for which it was used.

Robert Murphy, who had never ceased to grieve for his son, was buried in the same grave with him. Susannah Murphy was awarded £300 in compensation – the equivalent of two years' wages – after Harland & Wolff admitted liability for the accident, a rare thing in those days. Robert left his widow nearly £5,000, a huge amount. Perhaps he had been able to save such a sum on account of his being teetotal, but it still wasn't enough to enable her to continue to live in the family house. Susannah moved into a smaller place, where she remained until her death, aged eighty, in 1949.

Other fatalities also involved falls: Samuel Scott, a fifteen-year-old member of a riveting gang, fell from a ladder, nineteen-year-old John Kelly fell from the slipway, and on 8 March 1912 the *Belfast News Letter* reported a further accident with some machinery.

The services of the new motor ambulance were requisitioned for the first time yesterday afternoon, when it
received a call to the White Star liner *Titanic*, which was
lying in the new graving dock. It appears that a young man
of 22 years of age, named George Stewart, residing at 95
Mountcollyer Road, was working on a crane when he was
crushed in the machinery. The ambulance immediately
conveyed the unfortunate man to the Royal Victoria
Hospital, where it was found that he was suffering from
severe internal injuries. The time taken by the new motor
from headquarters to the hospital was under a quarter of
an hour. Inquiries made at an early hour this morning
elicited the information that the patient was progressing
favourably.

Of course, any deaths or serious accidents incurred during
building works were abhorrent to the company and deeply
sad for the bereaved families. However, it must be said that
given the risks of the work, it is a miracle there weren't
more.

CHAPTER FIVE

PROPELLING POWER

From the middle of the eighteenth century, when the Industrial Revolution began, to the present day, progress has been most noticeable in terms of speed. Mechanization made it possible to do all kinds of things more quickly, from spinning wool to printing books. Eventually, those mechanisms that made life less arduous were developed to make life more fun. Engineers turned their thoughts to transport, and their inventions brought a revolution, not least in shipping.

ENGINES

Among the many innovations that occurred in mechanical engineering at the turn of the nineteenth and twentieth centuries, one that was to have special significance was the marine steam turbine engine. Essentially, a turbine is a rotary engine that extracts energy from a fluid, steam, or air flow and converts it into useful work. The simplest turbines have one moving part, a rotor in the form of a shaft or drum, with blades attached. The propulsive power – water, steam or gas – acts on the blades, or the blades react to the flow, and they move, thus imparting rotational energy to the rotor or drum. Waterwheels and windmills are simple examples of the principle.

The marine steam turbine was first developed by the thirty-year-old Cambridge mathematics alumnus Charles Algernon Parsons in 1884, when he was head of electrical equipment development at a ships' engine manufacturers near Newcastle-upon-Tyne. He first used his new invention to drive an electrical generator (also his invention), which made the production of cheap electricity possible. This was in itself a massive step forward, but it was the steam turbine engine, as a means of ship propulsion, that was to have a world-changing effect. In 1889 Parsons founded his own company, Parsons Marine Steam Turbine Company, to produce his turbo-generators, and after a modest start, rapid improvements meant that ten years later he had built his first megawatt turbine for a plant in Germany, at Eberfeld.

Parsons was not alone in his work with turbines. A close Swedish contemporary, Gustaf de Laval, had also worked on them. His impulse turbine worked by changing the direction of flow of a high-velocity fluid or gas jet. This, however, subjected the machine to powerful centrifugal forces. As the materials then available could not withstand the forces put on them, the impulse turbine had limited output. Parsons' reaction turbine developed torque (twisting movement) by reacting to the pressure or mass of the gas or fluid: gas, steam and water turbines have a casing round the blades, which contains and controls the propulsive agent. The Parsons type needs twice the number of blades as the Laval type, which makes it longer and heavier, but more efficient.

Parsons's ideas were as diverse as they were interesting. Among his inventions was a steam-driven helicopter that lifted itself several feet into the air – a huge achievement in 1893, when most engineers dismissed the possibility of mechanical flight. In 1895 he constructed a model monoplane that rose 20 feet into the air and flew for 80 yards. His auxelophone, for amplifying musical and vocal sounds without the distortion inseparable from reproduction by a mechanical diaphragm, was adopted by the conductor Sir Henry Wood and used at concerts at the Queen's Hall, London, in 1896. He also invented the first non-skid motor tyres and a means of creating diamonds artificially by crystallizing coal.

In June 1897, the year of Queen Victoria's Diamond Jubilee, he showed off his yacht *Turbinia* near Portsmouth during Her Majesty's Jubilee Fleet Review. *Turbinia* could make 34 knots – 7 knots faster than the fastest warship then afloat, though part of the speed was due to the boat's slender lines and relative lightness. He was made a member of the Royal Society in 1898.

Within two years, the new destroyers HMSS *Viper* and *Cobra* had been launched, each equipped with Parsons' turbines. The first turbine-powered passenger ship, a Clyde steamer, TS *King Edward*, appeared in 1901, and the first battleship, *Dreadnought*, followed in 1906. Parsons was awarded the Rumford Medal of the Royal Society in 1902, and (although already the son of an earl) was knighted in 1911 and made a member of the Order of Merit in 1927. His company still exists in Heaton, Newcastle, but is now part of the Siemens group.

Parsons may subsequently have regretted letting the Germans know the secret of his invention. *Von der Tann*, Germany's first battle-cruiser, was laid down on 25 March 1908 and launched a year later on 20 March. She was built by Blohm & Voss (now part of ThyssenKrupp) of Hamburg, and was powered by two Parsons turbines.

The engine that drove *Titanic*'s central propeller was a Parsons turbine as well, but in those days the turbine, though it already displayed considerable power for its size and weight, was yet to become an economically viable replacement for the reciprocating (or piston) engine.

Cunard, however, in pursuit of speed, had decided to switch to turbines in 1904, and the *Lusitania* and *Mauretania* were both equipped with them, the *Mauretania* being at the time of her first voyages the largest application of this new technology to date. (The two sister ships were the only ones to win the Blue Riband for Cunard and, indeed, Britain during the opening decades of the twentieth century.) However, during trials, the turbines caused significant vibration at high speeds; in response, the *Mauretania* was fitted with strengthening members and redesigned propellers before entering service, which reduced the problem.

While White Star was more concerned with economy, luxury and reliability than speed, they nonetheless wanted to keep vibration to a minimum, so they compromised and stuck to the reciprocating engine for *Titanic*'s main power, installing one for each of the wing propellers. But it was clear to the engineers at Harland & Wolff that the kind of power needed to drive a liner of Olympic-class size at over 20 knots (the *Mauretania* could make 25, *Titanic* 23) was beyond even the largest reciprocating engines, and they were aware of what Cunard had already achieved. So they met the innovation almost halfway: they'd have three engines, but only one of them would be a turbine.

Harland & Wolff had already obtained a licence to build Parsons engines in 1905, but since then, largely for economic reasons, had done little to implement production. Lacking both the necessary plant and expertise, and faced with a sudden need to produce turbines, it made a generous merger offer to John Brown & Company of Clydebank, who had built the *Lusitania*. The offer was accepted, and Harland & Wolff was therefore able to access John Brown's turbine technology and workshops, as well as a number of other assets belonging to that company. Following this, Harland & Wolff's engineers designed the turbines, which were made by John Brown, and then taken to Belfast for final machining and assembly.

Titanic's turbine was designed to take steam from the two reciprocating engines at 9 lb psia (per square inch absolute). It was among the biggest marine exhaust turbines ever made (only that of *Britannic*, her younger sister, was larger): it was 50 feet long, weighed 410 tons, and delivered, when running at 165 rpm, about 16,000 shaft horsepower.

In fact, the combination of reciprocating and turbine engines was a huge success. It had been tried out on two smaller, earlier sister liners, *Megantic* and *Laurentic*, in the sense that *Megantic* was conventionally powered, but *Laurentic* was fitted with two reciprocating engines placed port and starboard, and a single turbine centrally placed aft of them, which was driven by exhaust steam.

CAUGHT AT SEA

New technology helped both *Megantic* and *Laurentic* to play a role in the dramatic pursuit and arrest of the murderer Hawley Harvey Crippen in 1910. Crippen had set off for Canada with his mistress on the *SS Montrose*, after having aroused the suspicions of Scotland Yard in connection with the death of his wife. Unfortunately for him, *Montrose*'s captain recognized the fugitives. Even more unfortunately, *Montrose* was equipped with a Marconi radio, and the captain had a wireless telegram sent to the British authorities:

HAVE STRONG SUSPICIONS THAT CRIPPEN LONDON CELLAR MURDERER AND ACCOMPLICE ARE AMONG SALOON PASSENGERS. MOUSTACHE TAKEN OFF AND GROWING BEARD. ACCOMPLICE DRESSED AS A BOY. MANNER AND BUILD UNDOUBTEDLY A GIRL.

Had Crippen travelled third class, he might have escaped the captain's notice. Chief Inspector Walter Dew of the Yard boarded a faster White Star liner, *Laurentic*, arrived in Quebec ahead of *Montrose*, and contacted the Canadian authorities. He arrested Crippen on the latter's arrival, and the guilty man was taken back to England on *Megantic* to be hanged. As *Laurentic* was able to pass *Montrose*, it might be said that the turbine engine also played a part in Crippen's downfall.

Laurentic's performance was successful and confirmed Bruce Ismay's already solid belief in Lord Pirrie and Harland & Wolff. Work on the new super-liners was able to proceed (indeed it was confirmed even before *Laurentic*'s maiden voyage) using the same engine configuration and combination, though of course on a much larger scale, as that employed on *Laurentic*. Ismay's faith paid off. At the end of *Olympic*'s maiden voyage, Ismay, who had travelled on her – as was his frequent habit on maiden voyages – cabled excitedly to Pirrie: 'OLYMPIC IS A MARVEL, AND HAS GIVEN UNBOUNDED SATISFACTION. ONCE AGAIN ACCEPT MY WARMEST CONGRATULATIONS . . .' *Olympic* had indeed not only lived up to, but exceeded, expectations: the voyage had taken precisely five days, fifteen hours and two minutes, at an average speed of 21.7 knots. And her fuel consumption had been gratifyingly low: just 3,540 tons of coal.

The two reciprocating engines were giants. Each was 63 feet long and weighed 720 tons. They would have been lowered into the hull using the floating crane, the only machine big enough for the job, and installed by a workforce of at least one hundred men. The bedplates they were placed on each weighed an additional 195 tons. Along with its own fully equipped workshop, their engine room was sited immediately aft of the aftermost boiler-room, between watertight bulkheads K and L. It was 69 feet long. Either side of the engines, ancillary equipment was arranged. The turbine engine room was next aft, between bulkheads L and M, and took up a further length of 54 feet. As well as the turbine, this room contained, among other things, the main condensers, the evaporators and distilling plant (for the production of fresh water, taking vapour from the evaporators), and several pumps for bilge and other purposes. Next aft was the electric engine room, which housed the four 100-volt DC main generating sets, which ran another 66 feet aft to watertight bulkhead N. The tube for the shaft of the central propeller passed through here, through the next compartment and the last bulkhead (P), after which it left the hull. The propellers would be mounted in dry dock after the general fitting-out.

'Built of steel throughout, and for passenger traffic only, [*Titan*] carried no combustible cargo to threaten her destruction by fire; and the immunity from the demand

for cargo space had enabled her designers to discard
the flat, kettle-bottom of cargo boats and give her the
sharp dead-rise – or slant from the keel – of a steam
yacht, and this improved her behaviour in a seaway. She
was eight hundred feet long, of seventy thousand tons
displacement, seventy-five thousand horse-power, and
on her trial trip had steamed at a rate of twenty-five
knots an hour over the bottom, in the face of unconsid-
ered winds, tides, and currents. In short, she was a
floating city – containing within her steel walls all that
tends to minimise the dangers and discomforts of the
Atlantic voyage – all that makes life enjoyable.'

Futility or The Wreck of the Titan, a prescient
novella by Morgan Robertson, 1898

BOILERS

The steam power for the engines was generated by twenty-
four double-ended boilers and five single-ended ones.
These last were located in Number 1 boiler-room, the
aftermost of six. Of the other five boiler-rooms, Numbers
2–5 had five double-ended boilers each, and Number 6
contained four. Because *Titanic* was so wide, the boilers
were arranged five abreast in Numbers 1–5. Number 6 had
four, since the narrowing of the hull so far forward
permitted only that number. It was the double-ended
boilers that powered the ship. The single-ended type was
used mainly for running machinery, including the main

generator sets, when *Titanic* was in port. The double-ended boilers were each 15 feet 9 inches in diameter and 20 feet long. Each weighed 91.5 tons and held 48.5 tons of water. Their working pressure was 215 psig (pounds per square inch gauge – a unit of pressure relative to the surrounding atmosphere).

Harland & Wolff made the boilers themselves, but many specialist firms provided ancillary equipment for them. Given the complexity of this essential driving machinery, it comes as no surprise to learn that the chief engineer, Joseph Bell, was the second-highest paid member of the crew after the captain, earning £35 a month.

PROPELLERS

The propeller shafts were made in segments of forged steel, each about 30 feet long. For the reciprocating engines the shafts were approximately 26 inches in diameter with a 12-inch hole bored through the centre. The tail of each shaft (the part that projected beyond the hull) was encased in brass, which gave it a slightly wider diameter, though it tapered to 6 inches at the tip. The tail was designed to be detachable for purposes of inspection, cleaning and replacement. The wings that carried these shafts to the propeller attachment points were just over 12 feet above the keel and 19½ feet out from the centreline of the ship. The shafts were serviced with an automatic lubrication system.

The turbine's shaft was slightly smaller, being 20½ inches in diameter with a 10-inch central hole, and the tail-shaft was 22½ inches in diameter, tapering to 5 inches. This shaft left the hull 12¼ feet above the keel.

Each shaft left the hull through a stern tube, which was both a bearing and a waterproof gland. The tube was lined with an expensive, oily hardwood, *lignum vitae*. The propellers themselves were of two types. The wing propellers each carried three manganese-bronze blades that were rustproof and resistant to extremes of heat and cold. These were attached to a cast-steel boss by heavy-duty studs and nuts, and were of impressive proportions: 23½ feet in diameter with a 'pitch' (or angle of attack) of 34½ feet and a total surface area of 160 square feet. As yet, no precise record of *Titanic*'s centre propeller has come to light, but it was probably similar, if not identical, to *Olympic*'s, which was also of manganese bronze, though carrying four blades. It was 17 feet in diameter, had a pitch of 14½ feet, and a surface area of 125 square feet.

Once the propellers were in place, they were capped with a cone-shaped 'fairwater' to streamline the end, and all water-vulnerable joins were carefully sealed.

ANCHORS AND CHAINS

Although the anchors did not form part of the actual driving force, it isn't too out of place to discuss them here in a little more detail. The stockless anchor, still in use in 1912, was developed around 1850. Anchors were made of cast steel, and *Titanic* carried three, in accordance with her official designation as an emigrant ship. Two were located on either side of the upper hull near the stem, while the central anchor was in the bows (beneath the forecastle deck) and would have been lowered through a hawse pipe near the top of the stem, and hoisted overboard by a heavy-duty davit installed in its immediate proximity. This central anchor (previously met on page 84) weighed approximately 15.75 tons and was attached by a wire hawser almost 2.7 inches in diameter and 175 fathoms (1,050 feet) long. It had a guaranteed breaking strain of 280 tons, and, when tested, did not actually snap until a strain of 289 tons had been put on it. The hawsers and their attachments for the anchors were made by Bullivant & Company of London. The anchors themselves were the work of Noah Hingley's of Netherton, Dudley. All were of the Hall's Patent type, in its latest form. But the star was undoubtedly the central anchor, the largest in the world at the time. *Olympic*'s was even displayed at the 1910 Engineering and Machinery Expedition at Olympia in London before being delivered to Belfast.

'Noah Hingley's, the company responsible for *Titanic*'s anchors, also forged the chains that went with them. The so-called King of the Chainmakers, the man who led *Titanic*'s chain-making team, was Benjamin Hodgetts. He was born on 14 September 1850, and married Elizabeth Fendall at Dudley Parish Church on 15 April 1872. They set up house at 4 Long Row, off High Town, and had nine children, five boys and four girls – the eldest was Joseph, born in 1873. Another son, Benjamin, had thirty-five grandchildren, of whom some are still with us today. Hodgetts thrived and went into property, buying numbers 2, 4, 6, 8 and 10 on what was then called the High Street in Cradley. Number 2 had been a grocer's, but Hodgetts, a part-time butcher, built a slaughterhouse and turned the shop into a butcher's. He died at the age of seventy-five in 1926.'

The side (bower) anchors were housed neatly in their hawse pipes to port and starboard. Smaller than the central anchor, they each weighed just over 7.75 tons and were held by stud-link chains just over 3¼ inches in diameter, with a length of 165 fathoms (990 feet). To complement this set, *Titanic* also carried two smaller iron kedge anchors for emergency use – to warp the ship around, or to act as hauling points if the ship ran aground. These two weighed 25 cwt and 12 cwt.

The anchors depended upon hawsers or chains – cables, as the latter are called in nautical terms. Hingley's also made the chains for the Olympic class. Chain cables were made of wrought iron, which is not only ductile but can be joined together in segments by heating until red hot and then fused by hammering – a kind of proto-welding. Mild-steel studs or crossbars could be inserted across the centre of each link for additional strength.

ANCHORS AWEIGH

The doyen of *Titanic* experts, Bruce Beveridge, has unearthed an eyewitness account from a worker at Hingley's in a local newspaper, the *Black Country Bugle*. The worker, W. G. Morgan, describes how the *Olympic* anchor was transported, and also alludes to the testing process. *Titanic's* anchor would have been treated in much the same way.

The parts were then transported to Lloyd's Proving House to be assembled under the supervision of Mr. Norman. I took part in this operation. The anchor now had to be lifted onto the test bed and a stronger chain had to be fitted to the crane which had to be ballasted with pig iron to counterbalance the weight of the anchor. Steam was raised to a critical point for the operation. Henry Green was the supervisor at the Proving House and Job Garrett was in charge of testing.

Having passed all tests, it was taken outside and painted white. Now came the time to transport the anchor to the ship-building yards of Harland & Wolff in Belfast. The big transporters in those days were Bantock's and they arrived with a huge wagon and eight horses. The wagon was backed up and it was loaded on. The horses were unhitched and replaced in the shafts by six of Hingley's own horses. These were massive animals – each weighing over a ton. In front of these the

Bantock horses assembled in two single files on a long chain. They tugged the wagon up the incline from the Proving House where the Bantock horses fanned out either side, allowing the Hingley horses to pull the wagon across the road to the entrance of Lee's coal-yard. The wagon was then slowly turned to face up to Dudley. All the horses then took the strain and to shouts of encouragement they slowly hauled their heavy load to the railway goods yard for the next stage of its journey.

At the Belfast end, the anchors were loaded on to a seven-horse wagon and made their way to the Queen's Island fitting-out wharf. The hauliers responsible were John Harkness & Company.

The links were massive and the aggregate weight of a 165-fathom cable was about 960 cwt. The cables were stored in lockers beneath the steam-driven windlasses (cable capstans) which fed them through. Each link was about 3 feet in length and of massive general proportions. There were also numerous cast-steel capstans to take the ropes used for warping *Titanic* in dock or harbour.

It is interesting to note that a large proportion of the workers in the Black Country chain-making industry were women. They tended to work on smaller linkage chains (for dogs, for example) and also on specialized items such as handcuffs. About 1,000 tons of chain were made in the

Cradley Heath District alone each week, and women here were at the core of major strike action in the autumn of 1910. Light is thrown on this action in *The White Slaves of England*, a book written in 1897 by Robert Sherard, a friend and biographer of Oscar Wilde. Sherard uses the word 'slave' in his title because 'chronic hunger can bind tighter than any iron link'. Most women workers at the time knew exactly what he meant. Sherard notes that many of the women were over seventy and others were under fifteen, but they all had to work twelve hours a day and more. Those of childbearing age were usually obliged to continue working even in the last weeks of pregnancy. Overseers, who ensured that no one slacked, were known as 'sweaters'.

According to an article in *Industrial Workers of the World*, in 1910 there were about 3,500 chain-makers working in small shops, and it has been suggested that up to two-thirds of them were women. They earned low wages and could not afford to join a union because their money had to be spent putting bread on the table. But in 1905 a Women's Chain Making organization was formed as part of the National Federation of Women Workers. The main mover in this federation was the Glaswegian activist Mary Macarthur.

Macarthur, thirty years old at the time of the strike, was a seasoned trade unionist, women's rights campaigner and writer. She'd been elected to the National Executive of the Shop Assistants' Union in 1902, moved to London in 1903, and there became secretary of the Women's Trade

Union League. She went on to found the National Federation of Women Workers in 1906, based on the principles of a general labour union. In 1907 she founded the *Woman Worker*, a monthly newspaper for women in the trade union movement. It goes almost without saying that she was active in fighting for votes for women.

Prior to the strike, the chain-making industry in the Black Country was actually getting some attention from the government at the time, and negotiations were in train to regulate wages and improve the lot of the workers. But during these negotiations, employers complained that higher wages would make them vulnerable to foreign competition, encourage the faster development of mechanization and hence lead to job losses.

In the spring of 1910 a wage, mostly affecting the women workers, was agreed within the nationally organized board. The employers, however, almost immediately tried to wriggle out of their obligations and started looking for loopholes in the agreement. All sorts of dirty tricks were planned and implemented. As a result of this treatment, the women were galvanized into action, and a mass meeting was organized. The women voted to 'come out and stay out'. It was reported at the time that seven hundred women had downed tools. A fund was raised by well-wishers, which meant that the strikers were not forced to return to work by need. Among donors to the fund were George Cadbury, the founder of the famous chocolate company, and the novelist John Galsworthy, who described the strike in his 1912 collection of essays *The Inn of*

Tranquillity, calling the women 'the chief guardians of the inherent dignity of man'. When the protesters reached Birmingham, they were met by the Cadbury family, who gave each of the women a rose and an apple.

The strike went on for ten weeks and ended in victory for the strikers. The money left over from the strike fund was used to found the Workers Institute in Cradley Heath. The Institute, built for the benefit of working people in the area, was moved in 2004 to make way for a road that provided easier access to a shopping centre. But the strike victory of late 1910 changed the lives of thousands who were earning little more than subsistence wages, if that, and vindicated Macarthur's view that 'women are unorganised because they are badly paid, and badly paid because they are unorganised'.

One of the women chain-makers who went on strike was Patience Round. She was well over seventy at the time, and before going on her first protest march she had never left the village. She was earning about five or six shillings a week, but she had to provide her own metal (two shillings a week), and her rent cost another two shillings, so all she had left was at most a couple of shillings, and from this she had to support not only herself but her ailing husband. Since starting work at the age of ten, Patience had produced 5,000 miles of chain, making on average 1.5 cwt per week. In her whole working life she only ever took two consecutive days off.

CHAPTER SIX

THE AGE OF ELECTRICITY

ONCE *TITANIC'S* GIGANTIC propulsion machinery was in place, it was the turn of Harland & Wolff's electrical department to install the complicated generating and wiring systems that would turn the liner into an entity using as much electricity for the time as a small town. Each of the four main generators produced enough power to run 100 present-day houses, and *Titanic's* total output exceeded the capacity of most contemporary municipal power-stations. When one considers how sophisticated the ship's electrical arrangements were even by today's standards, it is hard to believe that electric power per se was still a new thing, but *Titanic* was in every sense at the cutting edge of – and in many ways a showcase for – all that was absolutely up to date in 1911.

By *Titanic's* day, electricity for lighting had become a necessity for safety and comfort on all ships of any size, and was essential to most of the communications and safety lighting systems on board. It was vital, therefore, that it be properly maintained and safeguarded. To achieve this, a highly specialized team was recruited, as shipboard electrical systems were markedly different from those used on land. At a time when electricity was far from available to everyone, the liner was as well equipped as the most luxurious London, Paris or New York hotel. She had the two largest oven-ranges in the world, four lifts, and electric lighting, heating and ventilation in all staterooms. The kitchens were electrically powered right down to sorbet-makers, toasters and potato-peeling machines, and in the gymnasium there were two electric exercise 'horses' (one equipped with a side-saddle attachment for ladies) and even an electric 'camel'. The Turkish bath was run on electricity and featured an electric bath, a bit like a modern tanning bed, which even sophisticated first-class passengers viewed with suspicion (more details of this on page 232).

GENERATORS

The main generating plant's four 400-kilowatt dynamos were made by W. H. Allen, Son & Company of Bedford. Combined, they were capable of producing 16,000 amps at 100 volts DC. The four were arranged in two pairs fore and aft, with the crankshafts of each in line. Dynamos 1 and 2 were on the starboard side, 3 and 4 on the port, and they were separated by a maintenance platform. All the dynamos were steam-driven, as were the two emergency sets situated in the turbine engine room, by a set of high-speed reciprocating engines.

The four main dynamos worked in tandem, so they could combine output to deal with increased electrical load when required. The general arrangement was that one generator dealt with the liner's lighting, and two more with power and heating, while the fourth acted as a back-up. Each could be operated at varying speeds, and stopped or started independently of the others. Instructions were communicated to the electrical engineer on duty by means of a signal lightboard in the centre of the electrical engine room. The orders START/STOP and RAISE/LOWER, referring to speed, together with a number indicating which dynamo was meant, gave the engineer all the information he needed.

The main switchgear was located on the Orlop deck, just above the forward end of the electrical engine room. There were two main circuits, one for lighting and one for general power. The switches had a four-way system to allow any one dynamo to be allocated to any task. When demand was low, for example at night, fewer dynamos were needed, and some could be closed down and placed on standby. Again, specialist firms were subcontracted by Harland & Wolff to supply the necessary machinery. In the case of the switchgear, that firm was Dorman & Smith of Manchester.

DISTRIBUTION

Dorman & Smith also supplied the feeder switchboard, the main distribution panel routing electricity to all parts of the ship as required. It had twenty-five panels on each of which two circuits were controlled, and each circuit had a capacity of 600 amps. From here, forty-eight cables ran to master fuse-boxes distributed throughout the ship, and from these ran the individual circuit cables. In turn, these ran along the principal passages of each deck to distribution boxes, whence the individual cables carrying current to the lighting, motors, heaters and so on led off. Three main circuits governed the forward, midships and after sections of the liner, the first covering crew accommodation and mess rooms, as well as various stores and the chain lockers, the second-class passenger accommodation and also galleys, the restaurant, the saloons and other public rooms. The after circuit governed more passenger accommodation, stewards' and stewardesses' quarters and saloons, and so forth. But this is only a glimpse of the complexity of the entire rig.

While impressive, none of this was new. White Star's first *Majestic* of 1890 already had a very complex electrical system, but nothing before had ever been undertaken on quite the scale of the Olympic-class liners. There were 200 miles of electrical cable running throughout *Titanic*, and she was illuminated by 10,000 light bulbs.

Circuits could be split to serve quite separate areas – staterooms, public rooms, crew's quarters, engine rooms – and even individual motors were designed to be independent, and could be switched off or shut down as the need arose. One very important individual circuit was that governing the navigational lamps, each fitted with a 32-candle-power double-filament bulb, specially made by W. H. Allen. These were the forward masthead light, and the port and starboard sidelights, one on either side of the extremes of the bridge wings. They were coloured red and green respectively.

This crucial circuit also served the engine and docking telegraph lights, steering and standard compasses, and the Morse lamps. The fuse-box for this circuit was located in the chart room. If any of the navigating lights should fail, a bell rang automatically to alert the officer of the watch, and an indicator board showed which light had gone.

Many of the specialist lamps and indicators would have been supplied by William McGeoch & Company of Glasgow and Birmingham. These would have included bulkhead lights, deck lights, and lights illuminating such areas as the boiler and engine rooms, as well as the crew's quarters. For the passengers, even those in third class, more decorative lighting was installed by such companies as Perry's of Grafton Street and Burt's of Wardour Street. Each stateroom had at least one lamp, either in the ceiling or over the mirror, with switches placed in the most convenient location for the occupant to reach from the berth (or, in the case of the grandest staterooms, the bed). The grander cabins and suites had sockets for extra lighting or electric fans; there was a call-button to summon the steward, several switches with which to control the lighting from various points, and, in addition to an overhead light, there were wall brackets, and a reading light over the berth with its own switch. Individual cabin lighting had to be available on a twenty-four-hour basis, and several lights were required to be kept burning all night in public rooms, along corridors and on deck. Corridors were lit by pendant lamps set at roughly 9-foot intervals along the ceilings.

HEATING, VENTILATION AND REFRIGERATION

Heating was also governed by electricity, and electric radiators in upper-class cabins could be controlled individually. Heating was also provided by fans sucking air from outside over bundles of steam tubes. The heated air was then distributed to the various public and staterooms via ducts. But, of course, it was not possible to regulate such a supply of heat according to individual requirements. In the best first-class staterooms and public rooms fireplaces were installed and given the appearance of being functional by ceramic 'coal' in the grates, which appeared to burn, though the actual source of heat was provided by electricity. There was only one fireplace on *Titanic* that really functioned, fuelled with coal, and it was in the first-class smoking room. Its chimney rose vertically to the top of the deck-house roofs, where it made a 90-degree turn; the smoke was then sucked forward to enter the after side of Number 4 funnel, whence it was sent heavenwards.

Ventilation too depended on electricity to a large extent. Much ventilation was effected by natural convection and the fact that hot air rises, but this was supplemented by a large number of mechanical fans, rather like extractor fans, that worked on the centrifugal principle. These Sirocco fans were supplied by Davidson & Company of Belfast, and were driven electrically. Individual electric fans were provided in upper-class cabins, and additional fans were mounted on bulkheads in public rooms and elsewhere.

Electricity was also essential to the refrigeration plant. Even on such a short voyage as the five-day crossing of the Atlantic, a vast amount of food and drink – enough for up to three thousand people – needed to be stored, not to mention fresh flowers for the public rooms and restaurants. *Titanic* carried 6,000 lb of butter, for example, and 75,000 lb of beef. There were refrigerators, freezers and a thawing room, and the logistics of running them must have been nightmarish, but the system worked efficiently. In fact, there were four refrigeration units, of which half the total capacity was usually sufficient to supply one crossing, and if the reserve section weren't broached, its contents would still be usable. In addition to this plant, supplied by J. & E. Hall of Kent, there were two ice-making machines, with an adjacent ice room for storage.

COMMUNICATION SYSTEMS

Titanic's telephone system, the Marconi radio operating room, elements of steering and all the ship's telegraph equipment all broadly depended on electricity. Loudspeaker telephones, supplied by Alfred Graham & Company, were installed in noisy areas such as boiler and engine rooms, in the wheelhouse, and on deck, where they were placed on stands inside protective brass boxes. These consisted of a central tube for speaking, and two receivers, one on either side and one for each ear, which were raised into position when the phone was in operation, and pushed down the sides when not in use. The main points of contact connected the wheelhouse with the reciprocating engine room, the forecastle deck, the crow's nest and the docking bridge; the chief engineer's quarters with the reciprocating engine room; and the reciprocating engine room with the boiler-rooms. There were further telephone connections between the captain's and the chief engineer's quarters and the chief engineer's office, the purser's office, various senior stewards, the first-class smoking room bar, the first-class saloon bar, the surgeon, the Marconi operating room, and elsewhere. Calls were directed through a central switchboard – a sort of mini telephone exchange. Telephones on ships were still relatively new in 1911, and still had teething troubles, so *Titanic* was also equipped with two megaphones.

There were also cabin telephones, though these were for senior crew only. In addition to the telephones, messages could be communicated by means of pneumatic tubes that connected, for example, the Marconi operating room with the enquiry office that catered to passengers.

A recent luxury that also depended on electricity was the lifts – or elevators, as they were called on *Titanic*, after American usage. There were three in first class and one in second class, and they served all the decks that passengers needed access to. The second-class elevator was situated near the passengers' forward staircase. On *Olympic* it saw a good deal of use, but we have no way of knowing how much it was used on *Titanic*. The first-class elevators were placed side by side just forward of the grand staircase, and

THE AGE OF ELECTRICITY 133

were perhaps too discreetly boxed in, as they saw little use on *Olympic*. But people may have been disinclined to use them as they displayed a tendency to stick in rough weather, and as elevators were still something of a novelty anyway, perhaps passengers were just chary of them. The lifts were made by Waygood of London, already suppliers of over 150 lifts and service hoists to fifty battleships and liners, according to a contemporary advertisement of theirs.

Electricity above anything else made it possible for *Titanic* to give passengers the illusion of being on land while at sea. Virtually every creature comfort was available, right down to a ship's newspaper. The Marconi operators got news from their onshore colleagues, passed it to the purser's office, and there was a small print room where a news-sheet was compiled every night for distribution the next day. *Titanic* really was a self-contained world of comfort and efficiency.

PART 2:
LAUNCH TO
MAIDEN VOYAGE

31 MAY 1911 – 10 APRIL 1912

CHAPTER SEVEN

SAILING IN THE MODERN AGE

*T*ITANIC WASN'T JUST A passenger liner – she was also a cargo boat. Cargo brought in money just as effectively as people, and the White Star line was as well aware of this as any other shipping company, dealing as it did not only with the transatlantic route, but the routes to India and Australasia as well. The ship's title, RMS (Royal Mail Ship), is one indication of this. An important part of the cargo was mail, from and to the United States. In fact, mail, parcels and specie (bullion, coin and valuables) accounted for 26,800 cubic feet in the holds. *Titanic* not only shipped mail, but also sorted it en route, having an onboard post-room with its own postal workers – five clerks of the international Sea Post Office, three Americans and two Britons. These clerks were among the elite of their profession, as was reflected in their smart uniforms (they were sometimes mistaken for bandsmen) and high wages.

They were capable of sorting 60,000 items a day. Hours were long, however – seven days a week from 6.00 a.m. to 7.00 p.m. Loyal to the last, and expected quite literally to guard the mail with their lives, they desperately and futilely tried to drag sacks of letters to safety as the water inexorably rose around them on 14/15 April 1912. The two Britons, John Richard Jago Smith and James Bertram Williamson, and the three Americans, John Starr March, William Logan Gwinn and Oscar Scott Woody, all perished. A couple of days earlier, they had been celebrating Woody's forty-fourth birthday. But if their efforts seem almost vainglorious to us, it should not be forgotten that even the captain was under strict orders to place the safety of the mails second only to that of the passengers. The US Congress voted $2,000 each to the families of the three American postal clerks in compensation and in recognition of their heroism.

There was also the passengers' baggage to be stored: first- and second-class baggage alone took up 19,455 cubic feet of space. But there was plenty more stuff to pack in, including bales of straw, furniture, linoleum, machinery, barrels of mercury, oak planking, melons and other foodstuffs, and even cars. Everything had to be kept dry, and of course foodstuffs and anything giving off an odour had to be kept separate from the rest of the cargo and from each other. To add to the complication, parts of the cargo had to be offloaded at destinations en route, and various replacement cargoes loaded on. Packing the holds was therefore an exact science.

Titanic was fitted with eight electric cranes, two of which were capable of lifting 3,360 lb, the other six each lifting 5,600 lb. They were made by Stothert & Pitt of Bath, and electricity was the power chosen to drive them since they were situated close to passenger accommodation and needed to be as quiet as possible. The work of the cranes was supplemented by a Mannesmann derrick that swung from the after side of the foremast; this was stowed against the mast when not in use. The complement of loading and unloading equipment was made up by three steam winches and four electric winches.

Passenger baggage not wanted on the voyage was stowed in areas of Holds 2 and 3, and at the Orlop deck level it was packed into the space surrounding the specie room, which had previously been filled and locked. This was deliberate policy since it made the specie room impossible to access during the voyage – there was simply no way it could be burgled. Naturally, its entire contents went to the bottom when the ship sank.

FUELLING THE SHIP

Apart from the cargo, coal also had to be loaded. *Titanic* was designed to carry 6,611 tons of coal in her bunkers, with a further 1,092 tons stored in Hold 3. It took 176 firemen to heave over 600 tons of coal into the 159 Morrison furnaces daily, and the firemen were relatively well paid (an average of £6 a month) in recognition of the hard and filthy labour they had to undertake.

Coal was loaded at Southampton, and Welsh coal was

preferred, being the best burning and most cost-effective. But there were complications here, because of a national coal strike. Some 30,000 Welsh miners had downed tools in 1910–11 over what they perceived as the need to regulate wages. A further strike ensued in February 1912 and spread nationwide. There were reports of hundreds of men being forced to seek relief payments – a number that grew daily. The *Liverpool Echo* kept a close eye on the strike, running a photo of a deserted Lime Street Station on Good Friday: 'owing to the coal strike the gates were locked, the place deserted, on what would normally be one of the busiest weekends of the year.' And on the same day, 5 April 1912, the paper reported 'serious rioting' at Pendlebury Coalfield, Manchester, after scab workers were employed to work the coalface. A mob overturned the wagons and the police were 'assaulted with stones'. Several baton charges restored order. Riots also broke out elsewhere, and at one point the 16th Lancers rode to the Wigan pits to keep order and tackle two hundred young men armed with sticks.

The strike ended on 9 April and the *Liverpool Echo* reported that 'work has now resumed at every colliery in North Wales', but added that there were still difficulties in South Wales, especially at the Aberdare Colliery, which stayed on strike. There were reports of skirmishes with police and 'cracked skulls'. The Minimum Wage Act, passed as the price of peace, at least conceded the principle for which the miners had fought. But for a moment it looked as if the strike and the consequent lack of coal might delay *Titanic*'s sailing.

In a letter to his American editor, the journalist W. T. Stead, who was due to sail on *Titanic* to take part in a peace congress at Carnegie Hall, expressed his anxiety: 'The general feeling of unrest which is surging over the world just now is disquieting many minds . . . there is a general conviction that the end of all things is near at hand. It is a mighty interesting time to live in, although somewhat trying to one's nerves . . . We have got enough coal in our house to last another ten days, and then we are done. If things settle down into something like decent order here, I think I shall start for New York on the Titanic, which sails, if it can get coal enough, on April 10. It will be her first voyage, and the sea trip will do me good.'

The mood at the White Star Line was a bit more desperate. One of its chief clerks, armed with a revolver provided by the company, was sent on a mission to recruit enough 'black' labour to organize the loading and transport of 6,500 tons of coal from the Welsh coalfields to Southampton, where *Titanic* was to take on the bulk of the fuel for her maiden voyage. The clerk's name was William Bull, and he never used his gun. It would have been madness to fire on a hundred or more determined strikers, led by the likes of Noah Ablett, an Oxford graduate and committed socialist, and strike leader of the Maerdy Colliery in Rhondda. As for Bull, he was hit on the head with a shovel during a scuffle in Southampton and treated in the General Hospital. He recovered, and was the last man to leave *Titanic* in Southampton, just prior to her fatal maiden voyage.

Coal was delivered to White Star liners by the company's agents and shippers, R. & J. H. Rea. The firm, which had an association with White Star dating back to the mid-1890s, started with a barge capacity of 1,000 tons. By 1911, following the change of port of departure from Liverpool to Southampton, its capacity was such that it could deliver coal at a rate of 4,000 tons in fifteen hours, a world record, though it meant back-breaking work for the poorly paid coalies.

Their income was also unstable, as recounted in recordings from Southampton City Heritage Oral History. Martha Gale recalls: 'Always the men were out of work, especially in Chapel [district]. My dad was a coal porter, he used to coal the ships. There weren't many people had permanent jobs then – it was casual. You were picked up one day and dropped the next. There was no unemployment pay in those days. I don't know how we used to live, to tell you the truth.' And it truly was filthy work too. In another recording, Frank Scammell said: 'My father was one [of the coalies] who had a bath every day. But I do know . . . for a fact that some of the chaps, some of the coal porters, used to come home and they'd have a type of a sleeping bag, as you'd call it today, with a drawstring at the neck . . . coaling a boat would take about four days and during that four days they wouldn't bath. They couldn't bath for the simple reason there was no hot water laid on.'

The Rea barges, after being loaded by electric crane at the barge docks along Berth 28, were then towed alongside the liner, which would have been boomed (swung) out about 20 feet from the dock to be coaled. There the coalies would shovel coal into buckets that were hoisted or winched to fellow workmen standing on platforms suspended just below the coaling ports in the liner's hull – near F deck in *Titanic*'s case. Coal-chute flaps were bottom-hinged to take a temporary sheet-iron scoop. Coal from the buckets was then poured down the chutes over and over until the coal bunkers of the liner were full. The bunkers themselves were arranged transversely and placed amidships in order that the gradual emptying of the bunkers wouldn't affect the trim of the ship by any imbalance of weight. After coaling, the ship's carpenter would seal the closed and bolted ports with buckram gaskets soaked in red lead, making them watertight.

NAVIGATIONAL EQUIPMENT

So how was the laden ship with all its passengers to be got from one side of the Atlantic to the other? The route was well tried, but busy. Collisions were not infrequent, especially in harbour, and there were natural hazards, chiefly fog, icebergs, pack ice and reefs. At a speed of 20 knots (about 23 mph), one needed to be confident of the road ahead, so navigational equipment was of prime importance. Luckily, the equipment installed on *Titanic* was the best and latest available, though one simple but crucial item was lacking where it was most needed on the fateful night of 14 April 1912.

Until very recent times, the fundamental piece of equipment necessary for marine navigation was the compass. The first truly modern compass-and-binnacle combination was developed by the Belfast-born physicist William Thomson (later Lord Kelvin) in the late 1870s. In all iron ships the binnacle, or compass housing, was made of brass in order to counteract the adverse magnetic effect of the iron. Kelvin's binnacle comprised a teak or mahogany box with a brass cover, and magnetic cells built in to counter any magnetic effect from the ship's hull. It also had its own oil-lamp brackets so that the compass could be read at night.

Kelvin, a prolific inventor, formed a partnership with the Glasgow instrument-maker James White, and their firm (Kelvin & James White of Glasgow and London) supplied *Titanic*'s compasses and binnacles, though White himself had died in 1894. Selling at £35 each, Kelvin's standard compasses were used on *Olympic*, *Lusitania* and *Mauretania*, among many other ships. The binnacles on these ships were usually electrically illuminated.

Titanic was fitted with four main compasses, which were located in the wheelhouse, on the navigating bridge, on the compass platform above the first-class lounge, and on the docking bridge aft. But in addition to these, various other forms of navigation were employed. The sextant was still used to 'shoot the sun' during daylight hours, and although this method is not wholly accurate, it could serve as a cross-check. Similarly, the ancient art of dead reckoning ('dead' derives from 'deduced', frequently abbreviated to 'de'd' in ships' logs) was practised by use of the sextant as the sun neared its zenith. The sextant was able to measure the sun's maximum height, and from that the ship's latitude could be derived. Dead reckoning gave the traditional noon position from which the day's run was calculated, and although bets were laid on the ship's average speed or mileage per day, it is a myth that she hit the iceberg because she was racing in an attempt to capture the Blue Riband. Speed was never a White Star Line priority.

Until the perfection of the chronometer in the 1760s by John Harrison – a thirty-year labour of love completed just in time for James Cook's voyage to Australia – longitude could not be measured with any accuracy. By *Titanic*'s day the chronometer had been a standard piece of maritime equipment for almost a century. It is basically an extremely accurate clock set to correspond with the time standard established at Greenwich, through which the prime meridian (0°) passes. *Titanic* carried two chronometers, as a failsafe, plus a number of electric clocks, whose time was changed each midnight through two master clocks, as the ship gained 35–45 minutes every twenty-four hours when travelling westwards, and would have lost the same amount on the eastward voyage.

Another innovation, also invented by Kelvin, was the motorized sounding machine, which measured the depth of water alongside the ship. For centuries, soundings had been taken by throwing a weighted line overboard at the bow and counting the number of regularly marked spacings on the line when the plummet hit bottom. Kelvin's machines operated on the same principle, but consisted of a drum wound with 100 fathoms (600 feet) of steel wire rope, at one end of which a weight or sinker was attached. A dial was connected to the drum, and as the wire was paid out and the weight sank beneath the water, so its depth was indicated on the dial.

WILLIAM THOMSON (LORD KELVIN)

Kelvin was another giant of Victorian technical innovation, who in 1846, after coming down from Cambridge, was appointed professor of natural philosophy at Glasgow at the age of twenty-two. He held the chair for fifty-three years.

Combining the talents of engineer, mathematician and physicist, he made his name in the fields of electricity and magnetism. In 1854 he published a paper 'On the Theory of the Electric Telegraph'; two years later he invented the mirror galvanometer, a system of receiving messages, and the year after that he helped direct the laying of the first transatlantic submarine cable. He became a consultant for submarine cables worldwide and this occupied him until 1879, but it didn't prevent him from working on other projects. He invented the electricity meter, and perfected (among other things) the ship's compass. He was knighted in 1866, raised to the peerage in 1892 and made one of the first members of the Order of Merit in 1902.

Speed had long been determined by casting a knotted rope with a log or piece of wood attached to the end of it over the bows of the ship and calculating the time (measured with an hourglass) that it took for the log to pass from stem to stern, a known distance. It was then easy to count the knots, which were tied at regular intervals and commensurate to fractions of a predetermined distance. In fact, the nautical mile equals about 1.15 land miles, so a given number of knots per hour is marginally faster than miles per hour. *Titanic* used a Walker's Patent Neptune Taffrail Log, 9 inches long and equipped with a 5-inch dial. Basically, a rotator, or mini-propeller, was towed through the water at the end of a line; it turned at the same speed as the ship moved, and this figure was read off the dial. It was more sophisticated than the original rope and log, but not much more. There was plenty of scope for maritime innovation even after the glory days of the great Edwardian liners.

More innovative was the system of submarine signalling that *Titanic* carried. A kind of proto-sonar, the system depended on the ship receiving the varying sounds of submarine bells that were suspended into the sea from lightships and intended for navigational purposes. Bells were also located by lighthouses and on a number of buoys. As reefs (and wrecks) were common near the US coastline, the system was a considerable safety factor.

The bells had been established by Trinity House (the lighthouse authority) in London and by the US Lighthouse Service, and were more efficient than foghorns. A foghorn's sound travels through air and – ironically – could be misleading in a fog, but sound travels through water 3.5 times faster than it does through air, and can be heard from further away. The submarine bells were audible at a distance of up to 15 miles, and their sound could be accurately pinpointed. They were sunk to a depth of about 30 feet, and their signals were picked up by two microphones inside the hull on *Titanic*, each located within small tanks positioned forward and below water level on the port and starboard sides. The listening operator could listen to them either together or separately. The bells helped to determine position as well as distance, since each bell had its own unique series of strokes.

It has been argued that *Titanic* was lacking one essential piece of kit at a crucial moment – namely, binoculars. Had these been issued to the lookouts in the crow's nest, the iceberg might have been sighted in time; it was, after all, a clear and calm night. Some claimed that lookouts generally did not use binoculars, and this was one of the contentions at the inquiries that followed the disaster. Senior officers were issued with binoculars, however, and an additional pair was available on the bridge. It further appears that the lookouts not only expected to have a pair, but were indignant to find them missing. The fact remains, though, that binoculars were available to the lookouts – pairs that were not at the time being used by certain of the senior officers – but that they had not been given to them. Interestingly, at the London inquiry, when Second Officer Charles Lightoller (a man of undoubted heroism and integrity) was being quizzed on this matter by Thomas Scanlan, MP, on 21 May 1912, Scanlan's questions on this issue unsettled Lightoller to such a degree that the commissioner of the inquiry (Lord Mersey) pointedly put a stop to them.

STEERING EQUIPMENT

Titanic was equipped with three helms, or steering wheels. The master wheel was in the wheelhouse, from where the ship was normally steered at sea. A second wheel (usually used by the pilot or in any situation where frequent orders to the helmsman were called for) was on the navigating bridge, just forward of the wheelhouse; and the third was on the docking bridge aft. (Navigating instructions to the helmsman, by the way, might seem confusing, as 'starboard the helm' meant 'turn to port'. *Titanic* took her blow from the iceberg on the starboard side: in an attempt to avoid this, First Officer Murdoch had given Quartermaster Robert Hichens the order 'hard-a-starboard', i.e. go to port.) *Titanic's* wheels were proper, solid ship's wheels, not the tiny little metal ones of today. The wheel pedestal on *Titanic's* navigating bridge was 2 feet 8 inches high and carried a teak wheel 3 feet 9 inches in diameter. The wheel in the wheelhouse was slightly smaller. Its shaft passed through the steering binnacle and was attached to the steering device.

The steering device was a telemotor manufactured by Brown Brothers of Edinburgh, and it worked on a hydraulic system, using a single cylinder forward and a corresponding cylinder at the site of the steering engine. An override restored the rudder to its central position whenever hydraulic pressure was removed. The wheels were designed to be capable of four revolutions in either direction, at the limit of which the rudder was 'hard over'. Electric helm and course indicators were fitted close to the main wheels and in clear view of the helmsman and officer of the watch. As for the steering gear, located under the poop deck aft, it was driven by twin steam engines. Great power was needed to shift the 101.5-ton rudder, which itself was thrusting broadside against a very large quantity of water whenever it moved. The spur-wheels and pinions within the steering gear assembly were manufactured by Citroën.

THE SHIP'S TELEGRAPH

Navigational and engine-room orders were, more often than not, transmitted by ship's telegraph. The equipment was made by J. W. Ray of Liverpool and was installed on the navigating bridge and in the engine room. Each was fitted with a double-sided glass-covered dial, and each had two handles, one either side of the drum. Those on the bridge were 20 inches in diameter, those in the engine room slightly larger, and they were mounted on pillars about 4 feet high. There were five on the bridge, which were linked to their fellows in the engine room, and the commands they communicated – which could be confirmed back – will be familiar: FULL and HALF AHEAD, SLOW and DEAD SLOW AHEAD, STANDBY and STOP (the top lever position); then STANDBY, DEAD SLOW, SLOW, and HALF and FULL ASTERN. On *Titanic* only the reciprocating engines were capable of driving astern; the turbine could not. There were also telegraphs communicating with the boiler-rooms.

Like all other ships of size, *Titanic* was required by law to be equipped with a set of steam whistles, used in general to indicate navigational intentions, such as overtaking or in fog, to other ships nearby. They could also be used for Morse signalling, and they were routinely sounded at noon each day. *Titanic* carried her (dome-type) whistles forward on each of the four funnels. Each set comprised three elements, each 'bell' measuring variously 9, 12 and, in the middle, 15 inches in height. The different sizes produced different notes, but they were sounded in unison and operated electrically by a central control valve. The whistles for *Titanic* were supplied by Smith Brothers of Hyson Green, Nottingham.

Also included was a full complement of flags, variously for company identification, signalling and dressing. Since Captain Smith was a member of the Royal Naval Reserve, he was entitled to wear (i.e. fly) the Blue Ensign (as opposed to the Red) at the stern. *Titanic* also flew the White Star pennant, swallow-tailed and 3 yards long, displaying a white star on a red ground, from her mainmast, and also a Royal Mail pennant when leaving Southampton and entering ports of call. The Blue Peter, a square or rectangular blue flag with a white square or rectangle at its centre, was flown to indicate that a ship's departure was imminent. The practice goes back to the late eighteenth century, when the British Navy used it as a signal to any not yet aboard to join ship. The origins of the nickname 'Blue Peter' are uncertain. A pilot flag would also be worn when the pilot was on board in British waters, since, despite her American ownership, *Titanic* was deemed to be a British ship, registered as she was at Liverpool.

While flags could be used to signal to other ships, Morse code was used too, both telegraphically and by means of electric signal lights. *Titanic* carried two such lights, fitted to the roof of the port and starboard navigating bridge wings. The lamps stood 65 feet above the water and were fitted with special lenses and bulbs of up to 50 candlepower, so they could be seen from a great distance at night when the internal lights of the navigating bridge were routinely darkened. They were operated from within the bridge. In addition to these, a range of rockets and flares was carried for signalling, flares being especially useful for deployment in lifeboats following a wreck. *Titanic*'s rockets were capable of reaching 800 feet, leaving a comet-like tail behind them, and at their zenith bursting into a scattering of white stars. The altitude they reached meant that the explosion could be seen by a ship even over the curve of the horizon. However, rockets (usually coloured) were also used as company-identifying signals at night between ships, and as these could be confused with distress signals, the habit was developed of adopting white-star-producing rockets exclusively to indicate distress.

'Particular attention is to be devoted to the arrangement of flags so that when flying they will have a symmetrical appearance. The flags should be evenly spaced and the same number of square flags between pendants. Since there are only two burgees in the International Code the best position for them is at each end of the line. The appearance of a string of flags is often completely spoilt by the line sagging in the middle. It is hard to avoid such an occurrence when flags are merely toggled together, but may be successfully overcome by fitting dressing lines. These lines may be made of light wire or small manila. The flags are seized to the lines, the middle of the hoist being secured to the line with a whipping of sailmaker's twine. When seizing the flags to the line, the utmost care is to be taken to ensure the flags are evenly spaced; holidays between flags spoil the effect. If manila rope is used, be sure the rope is thoroughly stretched before setting up otherwise sagging is sure to come.

'The order of flags may be left to the discretion of the responsible officer. The ensign is carried in its proper place. No ensigns of any kind are to be used in dressing lines.'

Brown's Signalling, 1908

THE MARCONI OPERATORS

Morse was also the method of signalling by radio telegraph. On *Titanic* the two operators responsible for it were Jack

Phillips, who was to go down with the ship, and his assistant, Harold Bride, who survived. At the time of the disaster, Phillips was twenty-five years old and Bride, twenty-two. Although they had the status of junior officers and had signed the ship's Articles, they were not crew members per se but employees of the Marconi Company. However, they were paid by the White Star Line – £4 5s per voyage for Phillips and £2 2s 6d for Bride. The men were adept at their job. Marconi operators were expected to reach a norm in Morse of 25 words per minute, sending and receiving. Bride could do 26, but Phillips was capable of 39 – an extraordinary speed. Operators were sometime nicknamed 'Sparks' from the electric flash of the Morse key, and Phillips, whose hand flew when he was operating, was no exception.

Between them, Phillips and Bride maintained a twenty-four-hour service (no radio operating room on any ship was at the time required to do so, though this would change in the wake of the disaster), but the main purpose of their job was not primarily connected with the safety of the ship. It was to relay messages (Marconigrams) between passengers and their friends ashore, and to gather news from land for the ship's newspaper, the *Atlantic Daily Bulletin*. The Marconi installation existed principally for the benefit of passengers, and professional ship traffic did not take precedence, though the operators did endeavour to relay professional messages when they could. The radio operator on the *Californian*, Cyril Evans, sent warnings of ice to *Titanic*, and reported that his own ship, a bare 20 miles away, was stopped by ice floes. This was in the wake of earlier warnings he'd transmitted to Bride, who had in turn reported them to *Titanic*'s bridge. But when Evans sent his later message, Phillips was on duty, and working through a backlog of personal messages that he was transmitting to the wireless station at Cape Race, Newfoundland, 800 miles away. The relative closeness of the two ships made Evans's message to Phillips very loud in the latter's headphones – both operators were using spark-gap wireless sets whose signals bled across the spectrum and were impossible to tune out. But Evans's message cut across another signal Phillips was in the process of receiving from the land, and *Titanic*'s operator irritably signalled back, 'Shut up! Shut up! I'm working Cape Race.' Evans continued to listen for a while longer, but at 11.30 p.m. he shut down and went to bed. Ten minutes later *Titanic* struck the iceberg, but as *Californian*'s captain and radio operator had retired for the night, there was no one awake to receive the distress signals *Titanic*'s Marconi operators started to transmit thirty-five minutes later. Oddly, no one on the Titanic's bridge seems to have paid much attention to Evans's previous warnings, conveyed to them by Bride.

Titanic's radio call-sign was MDY. One of the very first standard international distress calls ever sent from a ship by radio happened in 1903, and used the newly created Marconi code CQD. CQ, sometimes transliterated as 'seek you', was the warning signal to stop all other transmission and pay attention. D was the code letter for distress. This

GUGLIELMO MARCONI (1874–1937)

The man behind the development of wireless communication was Guglielmo Marconi. Born in Bologna of Italian/Irish parents, he went to Bologna University to study physical and electrical science, and was soon improving earlier attempts to make use of Hertzian waves (a form of electromagnetic wave identified by the German physicist Heinrich Hertz in 1886). He submitted his findings to the British government, which responded quickly and positively, and in 1897 the Marconi Wireless Telegraph Company was founded in Essex. From here, in 1899, he succeeded in sending signals across the Channel, and he later managed to establish communication between Cornwall and Newfoundland. Marconi went on to develop a military receiving and transmitting set that was used in the Boer Wars, but in the meantime he turned his attention to the installation of wireless equipment on ships.

As early as 1903 commercial messages were being transmitted to the USA, and in 1910–11 he invented a new valve receiver and a new detector, developed a duplex system of transmission, and installed his equipment in most large ocean-going liners. He was a joint Nobel laureate for physics in 1909, and was awarded the Albert Medal from the Royal Society, and the Kelvin Medal from the Institute of Physics. He was also made a senator in the Italian Senate, created a marquis by King Victor Emmanuel III, and a Knight Grand Cross of the Royal Victorian Order by King George V. He joined the Fascist Party in Italy in 1923, and in 1930 his friend Benito Mussolini (his best man at his second marriage) made him president of the Italian Royal Academy, thus elevating him to the Fascist Grand Council.

was the signal Phillips and Bride sent out. However, in 1906 the International Telegraphic Convention in Berlin created the signal SOS as an alternative means of summoning urgent attention, since SOS in Morse is quicker to send than CQD, and its distinctive three dots, three dashes, three dots are easily recognizable even to a layman. In 1908, SOS became the official standard distress call, but Marconi operators tended to stick with the old CQD for some time.

The story goes that Phillips and Bride were first alerted to the fact that something was amiss when they received a message from Captain Smith: 'We've struck an iceberg and I'm having an inspection made to see what it's done to us. You had better get ready to send out the call for assistance, but don't send it until I tell you.'

At 12.15 a.m. the captain himself appeared: 'Send out the call for assistance!' he said, and handed Phillips a slip of paper with *Titanic*'s position on it. After sending for several minutes, they began to get a response, but none within the immediate vicinity. In their enclosed operating room, they could not know that the *Californian* was actually within sight of *Titanic*, but they kept sending. At last, the Cunarder RMS *Carpathia*, which was 58 miles away, responded. By now ten minutes had passed. *Carpathia* was a relatively small and slow liner. She would take four hours to reach the stricken liner, even under a full head of steam, and of course have to be alert to ice floes herself.

The operators continued to send out CQD. Then Phillips leant over Bride, who was operating at the time, and said, 'Why not send out SOS for a change? It might be your only chance ever to use it!'

When, having come to the aid of *Titanic*, the *Carpathia* docked in New York, Marconi himself went aboard with a reporter from the *New York Times* to talk to Harold Bride, and on 18 June he gave evidence to the American Court of Inquiry into the ship's loss regarding the function of the wireless and its applications for emergencies at sea. But his real contribution was summed up by the British Postmaster-General, who commented, 'Those who have been saved, have been saved through one man . . . Mr. Marconi and his marvellous invention.'

Titanic's wireless was one of the most powerful in the world, and capable of communicating with stations up to 1,000 miles away. Although wireless communication was still a relatively new thing in the first decade of the twentieth century, technical progress developed very quickly, and by 1912 all major transatlantic ships were equipped with radio rooms.

On *Titanic*, the wireless room and its adjacent quarters for the operators were in the mid-section of the deckhouse, just forward of the elevator machinery housing. On the starboard side was the operators' cabin, with its mahogany berths and fittings. Next to it was the operating room itself, with the table carrying all the wireless equipment placed against the after bulkhead. To the starboard of this was the so-called silent room, designed to muffle the sound of the spark disc, which was housed in a teak case. The room itself was very heavily insulated so that the operators and those passengers in staterooms near by should not be disturbed by the noise of the machinery. There was no means of communication between the operating room and the bridge, so messages had to be conveyed personally or by note. This was rectified on *Olympic* after the *Titanic* disaster, and the designs were changed for *Britannic*.

The aerial was of the 'twin-T' type then commonly in use. There were two of them, and the T derived from the aerial's appearance: the crossbar of the T was formed by the wires stretched between the two masts, and the stalk by the wires leading up from the operating room to the crossbar. Most ships adopted this configuration, although there were variations.

'The wireless equipment of the *Titanic* was the most powerful possessed by any vessel of the mercantile marine and only equalled by that of the *Olympic*. Its generating plant consisted of a 5 kW motor-generator set, yielding current at 300 volts 60 cycles. The motor of the set was fed at 100 volts DC from the ship's lighting circuit, normally supplied from steam-driven sets. The alternator of the motor-generator was connected to the primary of an anti-core transformer and the condenser consisted of oil-immersed glass plates. To eliminate as far as possible the spark gap and its consequent resistance, which, as is well known, is the principal cause of the damping of the waves in the transmitting circuit, the ordinary Marconi disc discharger was used. This is driven off the shaft of the motor-generator. The guaranteed working range of the equipment was 250 miles under any atmospheric conditions, but actually communication could be kept up to about 400 miles, while at night the range was often increased to about 2,000 miles. The aerial was supported by the two masts, 200 feet high, stepped 600 feet apart, and had a mean height of 170 feet. It was of the twin T type and was used for the double purpose of transmitting and receiving. The earth connection was made by insulated cable to convenient points on the hull of the vessel.

'The receiver was the Marconi standard travelling band, or magnetic detector, used in conjunction with their multiple tuner, providing for reception of all waves between 100 and 2,500 metres. The multiple tuner was calibrated to permit of the instrument being set to any pre-arranged wavelength and further to be provided with a change switch to permit of instantaneous change of circuit from a highly synchronised, tuned condition to an untuned condition (for stand-by), especially devised for picking up incoming signals of widely different wave-lengths. By reason of its robust nature the magnetic detector could be employed permanently connected to the transmitting aerial, thus dispensing with all mechanical change-over switching arrangements.'

Marconigraph, the house magazine of the Marconi company, May 1912

LIFEBOATS

In March 1886, a committee was set up by the Board of Trade to investigate the question of lifeboats and other life-saving devices, such as rafts, lifebelts, lifebuoys and life-jackets, and to come up with a minimum safety standard for merchant vessels. The standards arrived at were updated significantly in 1894, and further modifications were made between then and 1906, but they were left behind by ships the size of the big Cunarders and the even bigger Olympic-class liners. At the time of her sailing, *Titanic* certainly complied with all the regulations, which specified that vessels over 10,000 tons and equipped with watertight bulkheads should carry at least sixteen lifeboats. *Titanic* was well over four times that weight, but she did at least carry four additional, collapsible lifeboats, making a total of twenty. True, there were problems from the outset. Each lifeboat was supplied with compasses and lanterns, for example, but these were stowed not within the boats (for fear of theft) but in a locked box on deck. In the hurry and confusion of launching the boats in the small hours of 15 April 1912, kit destined for lifeboat use was not transferred to them.

The twenty boats were of three types. Fourteen were clinker-built and double-ended, fitted with buoyancy aircases along their sides. Measuring 30 feet long by just over 9 feet wide and 4 feet deep, each one had six cross-seats and could accommodate sixty-five people. The rudders were made of elm – a wood resistant to splitting – and were 1¼ inches thick. Outboard, they were slung with lifelines, or 'grablines', looped along the sides for people in the water to hold on to in case of need, and they were also fitted with a mast and sail. They were painted white outside and tan inside. Each lifeboat hung in its own pair of davits on the Boat deck.

Two more lifeboats were 25-foot cutters, about 7 feet wide and 3 feet deep, similar in form to the main lifeboats, but somewhat smaller. They each had a capacity of forty. These were carried near the navigating bridge, one to port and one to starboard, and while *Titanic* was at sea, each was slung outboard, ready for immediate use in case, for example, somebody fell overboard. Certain members of the crew received specific training for handling them.

The final four lifeboats were Engelhardt collapsibles,

referred to as 'rafts' by the crew, to whom they were new. The Engelhardts – a Danish design, and supplied by McAlister's of Glasgow – were indeed wooden rafts, boat-shaped, with heavy canvas sides that could be raised and battened to form a boat. They measured 27½ feet long by 8 feet wide and 3 feet deep and accommodated forty-seven people. Lettered A, B, C and D, they were stored in their collapsed condition, two near the cutters, and two on the roof of the officers' quarters deckhouse. Their addition to the complement of lifeboats meant that Titanic exceeded the minimum requirement by four, but actually getting two down from the roof and erecting any of them at speed and in an emergency does not seem to have been tried out. At the time of the wreck, the two Engelhardts stowed on deck were erected and launched without any problem. However, the two stored on the roof, over 8 feet above the deck, could not be properly lowered as the gear for doing this was stowed in the boatswain's store in the bows and was under water by the time it was decided to use these two boats. An attempt was made to slide Engelhardt B off the roof using spars, but the boat weighed 33 cwt and the spars snapped under the weight, causing the boat to fall to the deck. It couldn't be launched, but it floated off as the liner sank, along with its fellow unlaunched collapsible, and both at least served as rafts. Indeed, they had been designed to float even if they sprang a leak.

Each of the principal lifeboats was generally equipped as shown overleaf.

- 10 oars
- 1 sea-anchor – designed to allow the boat to ride steady with the bow pointed towards the wind and waves; the anchor was also fitted with an oil-distributor, which released oil on to the surrounding sea and calmed it (in fact, the *Titanic* sank in calm waters)
- 2 balers
- 1 rudder and a tiller

- 1 painter – essentially a tow-rope, 25 fathoms (150 feet) long
- 2 boat hooks
- 2 hatchets
- 2 x 10-gallon tanks of fresh water
- 1 mast and sail
- 1 compass (not in the event deployed, see page 162)
- 1 lantern (possibly also not deployed in at least some cases)

There were also metal provision tanks (boxes), which were watertight and contained biscuits. Some controversy erupted over provisioning, but the facts were confirmed by a survivor, Lawrence Beesley, in a letter to the *New York Times* of 8 May 1912, citing Charles Lightoller, the second officer who also survived. Beesley (1877–1967) went on to write a successful book about his experience, which was published just nine weeks after the disaster. In it he recalls how two women passengers from second class were prevented from boarding a lifeboat on the first-class deck and told to return to their own deck where they would find one waiting for them.

The two cutters were equipped in much the same way as the principal lifeboats, except that they carried only one boathook, one water-container, one baler and six oars apiece. The Engelhardts were similarly equipped, but had eight oars apiece and carried no mast or sail. They were steered not by a tiller and rudder, but by a steering oar. Oars on all the boats were made of ash and tipped with leather-bound copper. They varied in length from 15 to 12 feet.

The lifeboats were slung from davits designed and built by the Welin Davit & Engineering Company of London. Axel Welin himself had originally intended that Titanic carry thirty-two boats, and the davit design was so efficient that in fact the liner could have carried sixty-four. At the time, though, it seemed inconceivable that a ship such as *Titanic* could founder so fast that all the passengers would have to be taken off at once and at speed. The davits' arms were as far apart as the bows and sterns of the lifeboats they held, and could swing the boat out and lower it with the greatest of ease.

The problem, when it came, was not with the lifeboats, but with organizing a mass of people in the middle of the night, amidst much noise and confusion, directing them to the correct lifeboat stations, and, indeed, persuading them that the danger was real. Further difficulties were caused by the fact that many third-class passengers could not read English, so the signs were impenetrable to them; additionally, *Titanic* was so huge that many, if not most, of the passengers simply did not know their way about it, especially if access to lifeboats lay via areas of the ship normally out of bounds to them. Second Officer Charles Lightoller admitted that it took him fourteen days before he could confidently find his way around.

Titanic also carried forty-eight solid white lifebuoys (the ship's name was not painted on them – that practice came in only much later). Regulations stipulated that they should be no less than 30 inches in outer diameter and no less than 17 inches across the inside (which seems very small even for a modern supermodel). They were made of cork proved capable of floating for no less than twenty-four hours in water with a 32-lb weight attached. Additionally, six Holmes Lights were available for attachment to lifebuoys: when the lifebuoy was thrown into the water, its weight removed a plug from a copper cylinder, igniting the light within a minute of reaching the water. There were also 3,560 lifebelts, or life-jackets, made of cork and covered with canvas, which were placed in all staterooms.

'It may be pointed out that, of the six million passengers who crossed [the Atlantic] in the ten years ending June 1911, there was only a loss of six lives. The fact that *Titanic* carried boats for little more than half the people on board was not a deliberate oversight, but was in accordance with a deliberate policy that, when the subdivision of a vessel into watertight compartments exceeds what is considered necessary to ensure that she shall remain afloat after the worst conceivable accident, the need for lifeboats practically ceases to exist, and consequently a large number may be dispensed with. The fact that four or five compartments were torn open in *Titanic*, although no longer an inconceivable accident, may be regarded as an occurrence too phenomenal to be used wisely as a precedent in deciding the design and equipment of all passenger vessels in the future.'

Archibald Campbell Holms, *Practical Shipbuilding*, 1918

Once the fitting-out in the deepwater wharf had been finished, the ship was well on its way to completion. On Saturday, 3 February 1912 *Titanic* was towed to the dry dock, where her three mighty propellers were fitted and the hull was given its final painting. *Titanic* was then floated into the dock under the supervision of Lord Pirrie, and all looked set to proceed smoothly with the final stages. *The Belfast News Letter* published the following progress report on 5 February 1912:

The White Star liner *Titanic*, a sister ship of the *Olympic*, built by Messrs Harland & Wolff, was moved into the new graving dock on Saturday morning. The operations, which occupied about a couple of hours, were witnessed by Lord Pirrie, who was at the scene as early as nine o'clock. At that hour the ropes were loosened and three tugs –

Hercules, Jackal and *Musgrave* – towed the gigantic vessel from the fitting-out wharf to the dock entrance. A comparative calm and a good tide, high water being at two minutes to 11 o'clock, favoured the work, which was superintended by Lord Pirrie himself . . . Notwithstanding the vast dimensions of the liner, she was safely docked without so much as scraping her sides on the walls. The 'shoring up' operations were afterwards commenced and carried out with expedition. It then only remained to pump the dry dock in order to proceed to completing the furnishing and fitting of the *Titanic*.

Just a month after this report, *Olympic* was brought back to Belfast for repairs. This event was also reported in the *Belfast News Letter*: 'The mammoth White Star liner *Olympic* entered the new graving dock at high tide on Saturday morning . . . after her mishap in mid-Atlantic where she lost a blade of her propeller and sustained some slight damage to the shafting . . . *Olympic* reached the entrance to the dock shortly after nine o'clock. It was only a matter then of getting in, and so successfully was this accomplished that there was not even the slightest scraping of the sides of the vessel against the walls . . . Several photographers attended and took views of the vessel as she settled into position prior to the erection of the stays.'

This was not the first time *Titanic*'s construction had been interrupted by the need to repair *Olympic*. On 4 October 1911 she had been temporarily removed from the deepwater wharf to the nearby Alexandra wharf as *Olympic* needed repairs following a collision with the cruiser HMS *Hawke*. On 20 September, the twenty-year-old warship had collided with *Olympic* in the Solent, and the *Hawke* lost her prow. The subsequent inquiry pronounced *Hawke* free from any blame, and a theory was advanced that the great size of *Olympic* had displaced enough water to generate a suction that had drawn the *Hawke* off course. The navy too was absolved from any blame. However, the repairs were slight, and by 11 October the fitting out of *Titanic* was well enough advanced for White Star to be able to announce that she would set out on her maiden voyage from Southampton on Wednesday, 10 April 1912.

CHAPTER EIGHT

DECOR AND DESIGN

ALTHOUGH *TITANIC* AND *OLYMPIC* looked virtually indistinguishable, improvements and modifications were made to the younger ship based on experience with *Olympic*, especially in terms of first-class accommodation. The aim was to make the facilities even more alluring to the wealthy (especially Americans), who were prepared to pay very large sums to cross the Atlantic in style (see page 19). With the boom in industrial and technological development at the time, there was quite a lot of new money about, and White Star wanted to attract it. They made the key realization that the rich would want to bring their servants with them, and servants needed cabins too.

Lady Duff Gordon, who sailed first class on *Titanic* and survived the wreck, was charmed with her stateroom: 'My pretty little cabin with its electric heater and pink curtains delighted me . . . its beautiful lace quilt, and pink cushions, and photographs all around . . . it all looked so homely.'

The purser's office dealt with any requests, questions and problems passengers might have had. The chief purser was in a sense the general manager and chief accountant of the ship. Hugh McElroy, who had been with the White Star Line since 1899, held this role on *Titanic*. He and his staff were responsible for passenger and cargo manifests, crew lists and crew members' discharge books (a kind of personal logbook with details of past and present employment and status). He also had to be familiar with the entire ship, and more or less all its passengers. If the captain was the man ultimately responsible for sailing the ship, and the chief engineer was responsible for keeping it going, the chief purser was the third principal officer – responsible for the welfare, contentment and well-being of the passengers. Under his aegis, the enquiry office, on C deck, existed mainly for the convenience of first-class passengers. The office took telegrams to be transmitted, sold railway tickets and postage stamps, and could pre-book hire cars at the port of arrival – though requests for this service would have been rare. (The concept of car rental appeared soon after the advent of the Model T Ford in 1908, but rental companies as such don't seem to have appeared much before 1916, when a Nebraskan called Joe Saunders reputedly started such a company; Walter Jacobs soon followed suit, starting what was to become Hertz in 1918, but Avis didn't appear until 1946.) All sorts of other business with the land could be transacted via the purser's office and the Marconi wireless room. Currency could also be exchanged – the rate on *Titanic* was $5 to £1, a little above the bank rate – and traveller's cheques could be cashed. Passengers were encouraged to deposit their jewellery and other valuables in the office safe as theft on board was, unfortunately, not an uncommon occurrence.

The one external point in which *Titanic* differed from *Olympic* was the partial enclosure of Promenade deck (A), designed to protect the first-class passengers who used it from the weather. This was incorporated very late on, in mid-March 1912 at the earliest, and seems to have been almost an afterthought. It was not in place when the *Belfast News Letter* of 6 March reported excitedly on *Titanic*'s A La Carte Restaurant and Café Parisien: 'So popular has the Louis XVI Restaurant proved on her sister ship the *Olympic*, that in the case of *Titanic* this apartment has been enlarged and adjacent is a special reception-room for the use of passengers taking meals in the restaurant. The deck on one side is connected with it, so as to form a sort of balcony for those who prefer to take their meals in the open air. The *Titanic* also contains special suites of rooms, consisting of bedrooms, sitting room, bathroom and servants' room, and these will have their own private promenade, shut off from the rest of the ship, and not overlooked by other passengers.' These suites became known as 'parlour suites'.

Titanic's improvements meant that the overall number of staterooms was increased, and the parlour suites on the Bridge deck – the two most expensive and luxurious sets of rooms on board – were extended out to the sides of the ship and closed off to make two private promenades, fitted out and decorated in a half-timbered Tudor style, but with cane chairs and loungers. Aft of these on the same deck, on the starboard side, a portion of second-class promenade was converted into a French-style boulevard café, the Café Parisien, a 'charming sunlit verandah, tastefully decorated with French trellis-work with ivy and other creeping plants'. This led off the first-class A La Carte Restaurant, where the crème de la crème of the first-class passengers would take their meals; and it in turn was extended to incorporate a large, Georgian-style reception room. Similarly, on account of the larger number of first-class passengers to be provided for, the first-class dining saloon (where most first-class passengers would eat) offered extra seating. On *Titanic*, 550 covers could be served there at one sitting. This dining area was much admired, and the restaurant in the Grand Hotel Europa on Wenceslas Square in Prague is supposedly based on its design.

White Star backed this not inconsiderable investment with adroit and persuasive advertising. *Olympic* and *Titanic* were puffed as being 'without peer on the ocean . . . on a scale of unprecedented magnificence'. They stood 'for the pre-eminence of the Anglo-Saxon race in command of the seas' and were even viewed as contributing to 'the movement of the British and American people towards the ideal of international and universal peace'. And if this sounds not a little like hubris, two years before the outbreak of the war to end all wars, we should remember what pride often comes before.

FLOATING HOTELS

Olympic and *Titanic* were promoted to the wealthy as luxury hotels that coincidentally happened to be ships capable of carrying them between London or Paris and New York. The voyage was designed to be a pleasure and, where possible, create the illusion of not being at sea at all. In the best of the best first-class rooms there were proper beds rather than bunks, and every precaution was taken to avert any accident, spill or fall caused by the inconvenient rolling of the ship, which, in a really heavy sea, even *Titanic*'s stabilizers couldn't prevent.

One passenger recalls: 'We leave the deck and pass through one of the doors which admit us to the interior of the vessel, and as if by magic, we at once lose the feeling that we are on board ship, and seem instead to be entering the hall of some great house on shore . . . Great house, indeed – there was a hospital, a swimming pool, a squash court, a gymnasium and a Turkish bath, barbers' shops (which also sold souvenirs), a darkroom for photographers, a laundry and clothes-pressing room, smoking rooms, libraries, reading and writing rooms, lounges and bars.

On deck, of course, were all the usual games, including shuffleboard, cricket, quoits and tennis (high nets were erected to prevent the balls going overboard). There was also a game called bull board, the object of which was to throw smallish lead weights on to squares marked on a canvas-covered board raised at an angle to the deck. Indoor games included cards, chess, draughts and dominoes, but there was no billiard room as the roll of the ship, however slight, would have made play impossible. While card games were very popular, they also presented a danger because card-sharps had found the purchase of a first-class ticket a useful investment. The following special notice shows how passengers were advised not to play games of chance with strangers, as they could be – and sometimes were – fleeced:

> The attention of the managers has been called to the fact that certain persons believed to be professional gamblers, are in the habit of travelling to and fro in Atlantic steamships.
>
> In bringing this to the knowledge of travellers, the managers, while not wishing in the slightest degree to interfere with the freedom of action of patrons of the White Star Line, desire to invite their assistance in discouraging games of chance, as being likely to afford these individuals special opportunities for taking unfair advantage of others.

ONBOARD ENTERTAINMENT

Titanic boasted two sets of musicians – a quintet and a trio – under the general direction of violinist Wallace Hartley. The string trio played in the reception room of the A La Carte Restaurant. The quintet, consisting of string players and one pianist, played at fixed hours during the day: 10.00–11.00 a.m. in the after second-class entrance foyer on D deck, and from then until noon in the first-class entrance hall on the Boat deck. Later in the day they'd play from 4.00 p.m. for an hour in the first-class reception room, and for an hour after that back in the second-class foyer. They'd repeat the last two locations at 8.00–9.15 p.m. and 9.15–10.15 p.m. respectively. Their repertoire was light classical, jazz and ragtime. There's no firm evidence that, as has been claimed, they played 'Nearer My God To Thee' as the ship went down, but play they did, and Charles Lightoller remarked later that although he'd never been one for jazz, he was grateful to hear it, and for the calming influence it had on that terrible night.

Pianos were distributed in public rooms throughout the ship for passengers' use, and the one in the first-class saloon was used during matins on Sundays. Of the six instruments on board *Titanic*, the three in first class and the two in second were all Steinways. Four were uprights, and there was a grand (6 feet 10½ inches long) in the first-class reception room. The pianos were ornately decorated to go with the decor of the rooms in which they were set, having matching stools and their own reading lights. The maker of the sixth piano is still unknown. It was an upright, and installed in the third-class day room. It may well have been a cheaper Steinway.

'*Titanic's* professional pianist was called William Brailey. He lived with his parents (his father was a 'professional clairvoyant') and sisters at 71 Lancaster Road in Southport, Lancashire, where he was a member of the Southport Pier Pavilion Band. He was also a composer and had written an operetta called *The Fairies' Tribute to the Coronation*. In addition to the piano, he played the violin, the cello and the flute. None of the musicians knew each other before teaming up for the *Titanic* voyage, but they were professionals who were all acquainted with the White Star Songbook – a list of standards all musicians engaged on White Star ships would have been expected to know. These included 'My Old Man Said Follow The Van', 'Any Old Iron' and 'Daisy, Daisy', the last one a song inspired by Daisy Greville, Countess of Warwick, one of King Edward VII's many mistresses. (The countess supported the Cradley Heath women chain-makers' strike (see pages 121–4), and was one of the first [in 1894] to have her home, Warwick Castle, electrified. She was also not above attempting to blackmail King George V over her affair with his father, but in this she was thwarted.)

Brailey was also a keen aviator, to the extent of designing his own aeroplane. This, according to the *Southport Visitor*, successfully flew several hundred yards. In early 1912, there were only fifteen registered pilots in the country, and five of them were based at Freshfield, Southport's local aerodrome, which had five hangars, though its airstrip was the beach. Brailey was among the pioneer fliers at Freshfield, where he was acquainted with the famous local aviator Compton Paterson.

All *Titanic*'s musicians went down with the ship, fulfilling a premonition that Brailey had confided to one of his sisters in February that he'd be drowned at sea. The wreck also coincided with the date of his twin sisters' birthday. Among those who mourned him was his fiancée, a young Southport woman.'

LIFE ON BOARD

For all their luxury, the Olympic-class liners did not operate on a twenty-four-hour basis. 'Lights out' was at 11.00 p.m., when the dining saloons closed, though the first-class lounge and its reading and writing room stayed open for a further half hour, and the smoking room until midnight. In second class, the library and the smoking room both closed at 11.30 p.m. In third class, female passengers were expected to vacate the decks after about 9.30 p.m., and all third-class passengers were expected to be in their staterooms by 10.30 p.m.

To us these restrictions might seem severe, but the beds on *Titanic* in all classes were very comfortable, whether arranged as bunks or proper bedsteads, because many had horsehair mattresses on sprung bases, which were designed to cope with any roll of the ship. (Speaking of horsehair, 4 tons of it were used for upholstery purposes alone on *Titanic*.) And passenger space was allocated by decree: each humble emigrant berth had to be at least 6 feet long by 22 inches wide, and individually numbered. In the case of bunks, the upper berth had to be at least 22 inches above the lower, and the lower at least 1 foot above the floor. All passengers should have no less than 12 square feet to themselves, and no berth was to be placed in the vicinity of a lavatory. In first and second class each bed was allotted three blankets, two sheets and two pillows. Stewardesses and stewards made the beds in berth-style accommodation in such a way that the passengers would find themselves properly tucked in.

Mattresses in the upper classes were supplied by Marshalls of London – 'always soft, comfortable and healthy' – but Bruce Ismay wasn't happy about the beds on *Olympic*'s maiden voyage, as vibrations from the engines transmitted through them. He ordered that they should be improved. The bedsteads themselves, which consisted of wires and springs, had to be stiffened with wooden lathes. That solved the problem, but as Ismay later commented wryly, 'The trouble in connection with the beds was entirely due to their being too comfortable.' Otherwise, beds came in various shapes and sizes: in first class there were Pullman berths, which were upper bunks that could be hoisted against the wall when not required; and there were bed-and-drawer berths containing, as the name suggests, a drawer-pull storage space beneath the bunk (these were to be found mainly in ranking crew and officers' quarters). There was also a range of sofabeds in more modest cabins. Fitted as standard in staterooms were luggage racks, net wall-tidies, and wardrobes or lockers (in first and second class and crew accommodation).

For ships of their size, it might have been expected that Olympic-class liners would be able to take even more passengers than they did, but space allocated to public rooms and the larger staterooms, especially in first class, meant that they carried no more passengers than the *Celtic*, a much smaller older sister. *Olympic* was originally laid out to take 689–735 first-class passengers, 674 second-class, and 862 third-class, with the extra 164 berths forward arranged in the old-style, open-berth manner – true 'steerage', in other words – though these would soon be dispensed with altogether.

Second-class passengers could sample similar delights to those in first class, though obviously more limited. The cost of fares in each class ran through a great range (see page 25), and a few first-class fares were actually lower than some in second, but on the whole, second class on *Titanic* was commensurate with first on a good many humbler liners. The passengers themselves came from all walks of life and included professionals, civil servants, teachers, tradesmen, clergymen and the servants of the wealthy. Benjamin Guggenheim's valet travelled with him in first class, as did Guggenheim's mistress (in a separate cabin) and her maid; but his chauffeur, René Pernot, had a second-class stateroom.

'The majority of these [second-class] rooms are arranged on the well-known tandem principle, ensuring natural light to each cabin; the rooms are finished enamel white, and have mahogany furniture covered with moquette, and linoleum tiles on the floor.'

White Star publicity, 1911

Another good source of income for White Star derived from third class. Of course, people here had no access to the swimming pool or squash court, the Turkish bath or the A La Carte Restaurant, where one dinner would easily have cost more than their whole fare, but they were still far better catered for than on many other ships then. A good deal of publicity was directed at passengers aiming to travel third class, who were assured that 'in these vessels the interval between the old life and the new is spent under the happiest possible conditions'. Third-class passengers in the Olympic-class liners were generally divided among 66 two-berth cabins, 112 four-berth, 37 six-berth, 5 eight-berth and 2 ten-berth staterooms. The *Shipbuilder* magazine reported on the range of third-class staterooms on *Olympic* in 1911: 'They are mostly arranged for two and four passengers; but in some rooms six, eight or ten people can be accommodated. The provision of such a large number of two-berth rooms is an innovation, and should be very popular with this class of passenger. In addition to the staterooms, accommodation is provided for the 164 people in open berths on G deck forward.' These last would have been single young men, and their accommodation was considerably humbler, but they too had access to washing and bathing facilities, proper lavatories, and a decent amount of space. However, they were issued only with blankets, and had to use their haversacks for pillows. Still, the fares they paid wouldn't have covered the cost of two martinis five decks above them.

Third-class passengers weren't the only ones to benefit

from Olympic-class luxury. In the terraced workers' houses in Belfast that were dwarfed by the massive hulls of *Olympic* and *Titanic*, many otherwise modest kitchens had teak, brass and porcelain fittings either pilfered from the yards or taken as superfluous stock. And you didn't have to emigrate or have lots of money to go on to a ship. White Star didn't allow viewings of *Titanic* at Southampton because work was still being done on her up to the point of sailing, but day visits on board *Olympic* when she was in port before her maiden voyage were popular.

CLASS DIVISIONS

The open decks on *Titanic* could be used by all passengers (though of course divided from one another by class) to take the air. Most of the open deck space was available, with the exception of those areas reserved for officers and crew, and the Forecastle deck. Painted wooden or engraved brass notices distributed around the ship informed passengers who could and couldn't go where.

There were the three classes – three separate co-existing communities – divided one from the other and from the professional areas of the ship. Although in theory first-class passengers were free to go anywhere they wanted, and second-class could visit third, such excursions were not encouraged, and seldom was the right to them exercised. Class-division promenades were demarcated by gates that were never locked and seldom even had locks fitted, but they stayed closed, and the conventions of the time meant that people quietly respected them.

The locking-in (by closing Bostwick gates) of third-class men on the night of the wreck is the subject of controversy. Pro rata, more first- and second-class men perished than third, and more American males survived than their politer English counterparts, but the matter of the sinking is not within the scope of this book.

Those who did not feel like promenading, which was not only a means of taking exercise but also a way of socializing (much like the *corso* or *passeggiata*), could sit under a rug emblazoned with the White Star insignia on a teak deck-chair (or steamer-chair) and read a book, drink a martini, gaze vacantly at the sea, or doze. The best deck for both activities was the first-class promenade, which was wide enough to permit promenaders to pass chairs without the least difficulty. A chair could be hired in a particular place (designated by a number on the bulkhead that corresponded to one on the chair) for the whole voyage in exchange for a hire fee of $1 or 4 shillings. The hire of a rug was the same price.

Bruce Beveridge cites John Maxtone-Graham's *The Only Way to Cross* for the following anecdote: 'It was not uncommon for women with daughters of a marriageable age to choose their ship on the basis of its passenger list. The purpose of this was to book passage with a rich bachelor who would also be on board. After embarking, the mothers would sometimes bribe the deck steward for the location of the deck chair of their quarry, and attempt to reserve the position right next to it.'

In addition to the chairs, there were numerous

benches, not unlike park benches, distributed about the open decks, on the Poop deck, on the raised roof of the first-class smoking room, and on the second-class Boat deck promenade, for example.

INTERIOR DESIGN

Much of the interior design was undertaken in Belfast, Liverpool and London by the firm of Aldam Heaton, whose senior designer was Edward Croft-Smith. The firm had worked on earlier White Star liners, as well as on the Ismay family houses, but under pressure of time, much of the work was taken over by Harland & Wolff's own in-house decorators, who evolved a mixture of styles suitable to Edwardian fashion and taste – essentially rather heavy versions of multiple styles from Renaissance to Modern Dutch.

In addition to designers and decorators, cabinet-makers and wood-carvers were either employed or subcontracted by Harland & Wolff. Samuel Leith was responsible for tables, cupboards and cabinets, while carvers such as Leonard Waldron and Charles Wilson were employed to decorate wood finishings. Wilson made the clock surround 'Honour and Glory Crowning Time' for the first-class main staircase on *Olympic*, and carved a similar piece for *Titanic*. When *Titanic* sailed, her final fittings were still so behind that the clock for this piece hadn't yet been delivered, and a mirror had to be substituted pro tem.

Woodcarvings were naturally at their most ornate (modern taste would find them oppressive) in first class; in second class they were simpler and more repetitive, and in third class simpler still, yet 186 woodcarvers alone were employed on *Olympic*, and the same number would have been required for *Titanic*. Harland & Wolff had its own artists' and decorators' studio, which was responsible for panelwork, etched glass, and even curtain and carpet design, though some of this was subcontracted. Suitable genre paintings were commissioned for the first- and second-class public rooms. As in any great structure, land-based or ocean-going, every last detail needed attention – from doorknobs to lavatory pedestals, from upholstery to napkins. Belfast's linen industry did well from the napery and bedlinen departments. *Olympic* carried over 190,000 items of linenware and we can assume similar numbers for *Titanic*.

Carpets, cushions and other soft furnishings needed to be hard-wearing, high quality, and patterned so as not to show use. That rule still applies in any decent liner or good hotel today.

Getting the ship ready was a race against time and rivals. The German *Imperator* (see page 55), which was snapping at the heels of the Olympic class, had public rooms designed by Charles Mewès (1858–1914), the architect of the Ritz Hotel in Paris, which would make those of the Olympic class look almost cramped. Meanwhile, Cunard was already working on the four-funnelled *Aquitania* (45,647 gross tons weight, with a beam of 97 feet and length of 901 feet, driven by Parsons' turbines and capable of a top speed of 24 knots), which was built by John Brown. Designed by Cunard's chief ship's architect Leonard Peskett, who had travelled on *Olympic* and made copious notes, she was launched on 21 April 1913, just over a year after the wreck of *Titanic*, took her maiden voyage on 30 May in the following year, and stayed in service until she was scrapped in 1950. *Aquitania* was a real twentieth-century heroine, enjoying a thirty-six-year career (including war service), during which she carried 1.2 million passengers over 3 million miles on 450 voyages. Her faultless decor (designed by Mewès's business partner Arthur Davis, who tended towards the Palladian) earned her the sobriquet 'The Ship Beautiful'.

The intricate decoration of ships by real craftsmen – now a dying tradition, as witness the overblown yet suburban design of most modern liners and cruise ships – went back a long way. The form of a ship, designed to be buoyant, is in itself an aesthetic pleasure. When there was no straight-down stem but a proper prow, a figurehead adorned all important ships. Astern, the cabin lights were usually beautifully decorated as well. It is not known why in English, a language with genderless nouns, ships are always regarded as feminine, but it may have more than a philological connotation. As with other functional and fairly prosaic machines, such as guns, our ancestors lavished decoration of the finest sort on their ships. But that was in the days of wood. As iron, steel and steam replaced wood and sail, exterior decoration was lost, but the art of decoration was alive and well on the inside. In fact, you could say that decoration moved from the outside in, since few wooden sailing ships had anything but purely functional interiors, apart perhaps from the captain's cabin.

When *Olympic* was scrapped in 1935, it wasn't because she was clapped out, unseaworthy or unreliable. It was because her passenger layout was old-fashioned and modern passengers wanted, for example, more privacy and more en-suite bathrooms. We have to make some mental jumps here because what we now think of as standard, even in a modest hotel, would have been considered the last word in luxury a hundred years ago. An en-suite bathroom is one example, but it goes further than that. Even in first-class accommodation, many cabins were double-berthed, and that could mean (if you were travelling alone) having to share with a stranger. No hotel on land would offer such facilities to the rich or expect them to be accepted, but it was not unusual a hundred years ago on a liner. However, given the fact that once aboard there would be no escape for five days or so if on the transatlantic run, a lot of effort was put into the public rooms. But even these were somewhat restricted, most being only as high as the deck they were on, though the reception areas around the grand staircases were higher and surmounted by glass domes, as was the style in Parisian art nouveau brasseries, such as the Bofinger.

But that apart, by 1911 ocean liners in most respects outstripped all but the most luxurious hotels, and were not bettered even by them. To be sure, third-class accommodation was plain and simple, but the facilities offered – electricity, hot running water, flush lavatories – were better than those third-class passengers would have known at home; second class (one might almost say 'middle class') had evolved into something far ahead of what it had been in the late nineteenth century, and again facilities here were probably better than those at home for many passengers.

INTERIOR STYLES

Public rooms and staterooms in first class, and public rooms in second class, were appointed in a variety of period decorations. In order of antiquity they were as follows:

1. Renaissance style (c.1300–1500), with its taste for tapestries and rich colours, inspired some of the first-class staterooms and the parlour suites.

2. Tudor style (c.1485–1600), characterized by lavish use of half-timbering, was enjoying a resurgence of popularity at the time *Titanic* was built, as witness the many mock-Tudor houses constructed in the prosperous suburbs of large towns around the country. Oak was the timber of choice, and was used for furniture, wall panelling and beams. On *Titanic* the private promenades of the parlour suites were half-timbered in Tudor style.

3. Jacobean style (1566–1625) employed lots of dark wood, particularly oak, which was often ornately carved.

4. Mid-seventeenth-century style had a love affair with walnut, especially burr walnut. The furniture was still quite heavy, but now seats were upholstered for extra comfort. Veneers were inlaid with mother-of-pearl, and some furniture was lacquered in bright colours.

5. William and Mary (1689–1702), who came to the throne after the inglorious departure of the Catholic James II from British shores, brought in a lighter style, often using walnut. Antiques from this period were highly sought-after in Edwardian times, and their popularity led to the first-class grand staircases on *Titanic* being made in William and Mary style.

6. Bourbon style (1638–1793) originated in France and covers the reigns of Louis XIV, XV and XVI, who belonged to the House of Bourbon. On *Titanic* the three subtly different styles were used only in first class. The lounge, for example, was decorated in the manner of Louis XIV's palace at Versailles – masculine, highly ornate and very popular with the Edwardians. Several bedrooms were in Louis XV (rococo) style, which was lighter, curvier and more graceful. The palm court cafés on A deck took their style inspiration from the era of Louis XVI, which preferred straighter lines and fewer embellishments. The A La Carte Restaurant was decorated in a heavy Edwardian version of this last period.

7. Georgian style (1714–1830) was simple and elegant, perhaps best seen in the work of William and Robert Adam, Thomas Chippendale and George Hepplewhite. Walls and ceilings, often painted in pastel shades of blue, grey, orange and green, tended to have lots of decorative plasterwork, and marble fireplaces were fashionable. Furniture, often made of walnut, mahogany or maple, was dainty in comparison to other periods. On *Titanic* examples of this period can be seen in the A La Carte Restaurant's reception room, and in the first-class reading and writing room.

8. Empire style (French, early nineteenth century) was

introduced during the reign of Napoleon Bonaparte (1804–14). Usually massive, to match Napoleon's ego, furniture had highly polished veneers decorated with ormolu mounts (a bronze-gilt effect fashionable at the time) rather than carvings. On *Titanic* it made an appearance in the parlour suites.

9. Regency style (1811–20) is distinguished by light and graceful furniture, often in satinwood. Rooms tended to be brightly coloured and striped wallpaper became fashionable. This style was used in one of the first-class suites on C deck.

10. Victorian style (*c.*1820–1900) is characterized by heavy, over-stuffed furniture in dark woods. Inevitably, this style overlapped the Edwardian period.

In terms of decor, then, *Titanic* could be said to have suffered from a surfeit of riches. The parlour suites (see page 173), advertised as the last word in contemporary luxury, were fitted out in the different styles described above. Other suites of rooms drew on the styles above, and in certain cases even incorporated further variations dreamt up by Harland & Wolff.

Of the numerous styles, only six were used more than once. The Regency style, for example, was used only once – in the sitting room of one of the parlour suites on *Titanic*. Georgian style (specifically Adam) was used twice. Louis XVI style was used three times, and one of the bedrooms in this style had items specially made by H. P. Mutters & Zoon of the Hague, the Dutch royal furniture-makers, who were also responsible for several Louis XV bedrooms and the staterooms in Old and Modern Dutch style. Other staterooms on B and C decks were fitted in Harland & Wolff's own in-house designs. Despite the elegance of these historic styles, the interior designers of *Titanic* still succeeded in making the rooms of their first-class suites and the individual staterooms somehow heavy and crowded – at least to modern eyes.

Carpets in private and public rooms were provided by Axminster and Wilton, and manufactured in Ayr and Kidderminster. In humbler areas of the ship, and passages that took a great deal of traffic, linoleum (invented by Frederick Walton in 1855) and tile flooring was used. Such floorings were also used in galleys, pantries, bathrooms and lavatories, crews' corridors, and so on.

Curtains came in various styles, from early French (pre-Louis XIV) through to Louis XVI. Brocades and damasks were the most frequently used materials, and they served to soften the hard appearance of any metal or wooden surfaces, and add to the illusion that one wasn't on a ship at all. Of course, maintaining that illusion took special skill, not least because the ship's hull was curved and there was rolling to contend with. This meant that many chairs were bolted to the floor so that they would not slide about, and dining tables were fitted with flip-up guards around their edges to prevent spillage. Indeed, all joinery had to be made very carefully since there was nothing worse for the high fare-payers than the creaking and groaning of timber.

To continue the illusion of being land-based, ceilings in upper-class staterooms and public rooms had the appearance of plaster or stucco, and in a style appropriate to the period in which the room was decorated. The steel underdecks were coated in absorbent granulated cork to protect against condensation, then painted and covered with wood in styles ranging from faux-Tudor beams to plasterwork.

'Stanley C. Sutherland, who was born in south London and died in 1966 in the USA, was a tanner who worked on leather upholstery for the Olympic-class ships. His father, who became a wealthy entrepreneur through founding his Patent Impermeable Millboard Company, which reprocessed old newspapers, turning them into hardboard for use in house insulation, bought Stanley a second-class ticket on the *Titanic*, telling him that he'd meet valuable people on the voyage and make contacts who would help set him up for the future, but Stanley refused to go. He was in love with a girl who'd recently emigrated to New Jersey, but she wouldn't have any time off work until June, so Stanley didn't want to cross the Atlantic until then. He had a big argument with his father over it, but in the end he won, and didn't sail until he wanted to. Needless to say, everyone was later very thankful that he made that decision. Sadly, things didn't work out with the girl after all, and he ended up in Michigan as superintendent of the Eagle Ottawa Tannery, which at one point was producing 95 per cent of the leather for the car manufacturers of Detroit.

During Prohibition (1920–33), he used to order barrels of grease for the tanning process from Britain, and every barrel was accompanied by a barrel of Scotch.'

THE SHIP'S PUBLIC ROOMS

The pride of *Titanic* lay in its large public rooms. Even in third class, the day room was airy and spacious. The furnishing of the smoking rooms and drawing rooms on ocean-going liners of the early twentieth century were frequently subcontracted to ordinary furniture manufacturers, so occupants might well imagine themselves to be in any large drawing room or clubroom on land. (The smoking rooms in first and second were essentially male preserves, and their decor mirrored that of the great London gentlemen's clubs, such as the Reform, the Garrick and the Athenaeum. The reading and writing rooms were more subtly decorated, and tended to be the preserve of lady passengers. It was a period when feminism was in its infancy, and most people accepted certain separate areas for the sexes. It's amusing to note that – with supra-sexual snobbery – lavatories on *Titanic* were denoted Ladies and Gentlemen in first and second class, but Women and Men in third.)

'It is here [in the first-class reception room] that the Saloon passengers will foregather for that important moment upon an ocean-going ship – *l'heure ou l'on dine* – to regale each other with their day's experiences in the racquet court, the gymnasium, the card room, or the Turkish bath . . . Upon a dark, richly coloured carpet, which will further emphasise the delicacy and refinement of the panelling and act as a foil to the light dresses of the ladies, this company will assemble – the apotheosis, surely, of ocean-going luxury and comfort.'

White Star publicity, 1911

Wherever masts had to pass through public rooms, they were painted in the manner of the lateral watertight doors on passenger decks to conform with the woodwork and surrounding decor into which they intruded. All mouldings were screwed on from the back. As for wood finishes, all were French-polished (a technique involving the application of many coats of shellac using a rubbing pad). But in those pre-green days it wasn't uncommon to paint over even mahogany, as in the interior of the first-class lifts.

Equally, cabins or staterooms could be partitioned off by using portable bulkheads supplied by Venesta of London, especially in third class, thus creating smaller or larger rooms as might be needed, or converting passenger accommodation to freight use. It was also possible to convert certain cabins from second- to first-class use, and vice versa.

Decorative lighting in the upper classes was provided by two London firms – Perry's of Bond Street and Burt's of Wardour Street – who fitted staterooms and public rooms alike with a selection of wall-mounted lamps, 'electroliers' (electric chandeliers), brackets and pedestal lights. Many light fittings in first class were finished in ormolu and highly ornate. The candelabrum on the main staircase of *Olympic* was a particularly overblown piece of Edwardian design.

One of the greatest illusions was the grand staircase – there were in fact two of them, fore and aft – in first class. The main flight was marked by a central finial of a cherub holding a torch – to his left forward, to his right aft. The staircase itself went down as far as D deck. Even today one would find it hard to imagine seeing such a piece of workmanship and believe oneself on board a ship. But that kind of workmanship no longer exists.

SANITATION

When the Olympic-class ships were in the process of being built one could clearly see the builders' 'heads' (lavatories) off the starboard prow. These open-air facilities were in keeping with the age-old practice on ships. Even the *Cutty Sark* (in service 1869–1922) had no proper lavatories for crew, and passenger ships were scarcely better. Little wonder that 'ship fever', a form of typhus, was rife on even late nineteenth-century ships, especially among steerage passengers, and even on the relatively short transatlantic route. However, by the beginning of the twentieth century

Having been declared 'good for one year from today, 2.4.12', *Titanic* embarks on her first voyage from Belfast to Southampton, manned by a skeleton crew and shepherded by four tugs.

Life on board. Promenade decks, like many other areas, were divided by classes; here, second-class passengers make use of their deck. The opulent main staircases (*below*) were for first-class passengers only.

'The aim was to make passengers feel that they were in a five-star hotel rather than at sea.' Instructor Thomas McCawley (*above*) on one of the electrically powered rowing machines in *Titanic*'s gymnasium and a view of the luxurious first-class reading room, intended for use by ladies (*below*).

The wealthy were prepared to pay very large sums of money to cross the Atlantic in style. The most expensive and luxurious sets of rooms on *Titanic* were the so-called parlour suites, complete with bedroom (*above*) and sitting room (*below*), decorated in various individual styles.

An artist's impression of one of the well-appointed second-class staterooms (*above*) and one of the few adjoining, private bathrooms installed on Olympic-class liners (*below left*). Both are a stark contrast with the cramped, two-berth third-class cabins (*below right*), designed for women or families.

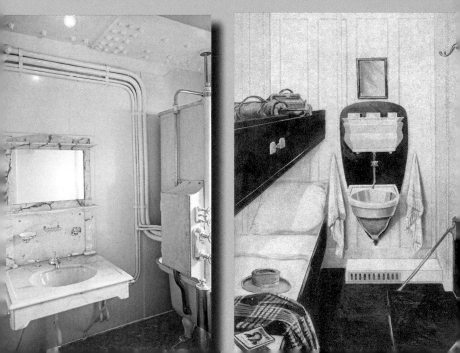

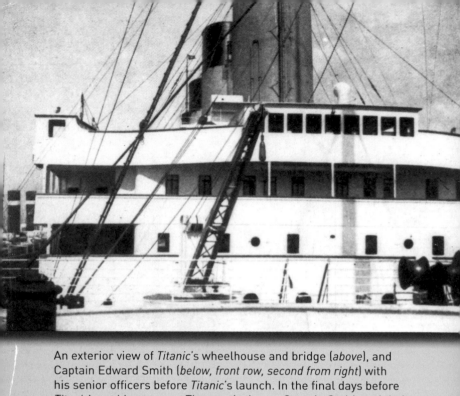

An exterior view of *Titanic*'s wheelhouse and bridge (*above*), and Captain Edward Smith (*below, front row, second from right*) with his senior officers before *Titanic*'s launch. In the final days before *Titanic*'s maiden voyage, Thomas Andrews, Captain Smith and their teams strove frantically to get the ship ready for her launch.

John Jacob Astor IV and others prepare to board the *Titanic* special at Waterloo station, bound for Southampton (*above*). Mailbags and trunks clutter the deck of the tender *Flying Fish*, ready for offloading (*below*).

The last picture of *Titanic* (*above*) was taken by Father Browne as the ship headed out into the Atlantic from Queenstown. She sank in the early hours of 15 April 1912, having struck an iceberg off the coast of Newfoundland. Lucky survivors in lifeboats (*below*) were photographed from the *Carpathia*.

laws were in place to guarantee at least minimum sanitary requirements for crew and passengers alike, and on the Olympic-class liners, Harland & Wolff provided cutting-edge sanitation technology. White Star was able to use this fact in its publicity: travel with us and enjoy all the hygienic convenience you'd expect in a first-class hotel on land. A further refinement was that electric lights in public lavatories were switched on automatically by closing the door.

Lavatories and their fittings were supplied by Shanks and Royal Doulton, well-established firms still familiar today. Upper-class tilework was supplied by Villeroy & Boch, a firm originally established in Lorraine in France in the mid-eighteenth century. Seats were generally made of mahogany, but also of oak and satinwood. During the 1920s and 1930s the seats frequently had to be French-polished between voyages as they were often scratched by ladies' suspenders.

Peasant emigrants had never seen a bath, let alone a flush lavatory, and they had to be instructed in their use by the long-suffering third-class stewards. Thomas Andrews paid special attention to designing out the nooks and crannies in third-class accommodation that its unsophisticated occupants used as impromptu lavatories. Nevertheless, many still deposited their filth in any available corner, and mopping-up operations had to be undertaken every morning.

Technically, what Harland & Wolff provided was a water-closet in a room that also contained a washbasin. These might be en suite, but not even in first class were private bathrooms the norm, and there were none in second class. For the average first-class passenger and everyone in second class, the procedure was to book a bath with one's bedroom steward, who would pass on the request to a bathroom steward, who then drew the bath and let the passenger know it was ready. In several more modest upper-class cabins the foldaway washbasin or 'compactom' was installed, a model also used on the railway. By contrast, luxury suites had double basins in their bathrooms, as well as proper baths. Fittings, such as lavatory paper holders, towel rails, soap dishes, and even combined cigar holders and match strikers, were supplied by George Field & Company. Luckily for White Star, sea-water baths were popular at the time, and considered healthy.

As for third-class passengers, they were limited in their bathing facilities as there were only two bathrooms for them on the entire *Titanic* – one for men and one for women. Most people travelling in third class would not habitually have taken a bath more than once a week, and the crossing was normally six days, so it may be imagined that few bothered to bathe at all. Third-class staterooms did, however, have access to pedestal WCs and decent enamelled washbasins set in slate counters. Throughout the ship there were public lavatories for ladies and gentlemen (or men and women) equipped with stalls, booths and washbasins. In facilities for crew and third-class passengers, there were washrooms with iron tubs for washing clothes. Upper-class passengers would use the ship's laundry.

CHAPTER NINE

FOOD AND DRINK

WHEN *TITANIC* WAS BUILT, her kitchens were considered the best in the world for an ocean liner. Apart from the A La Carte Restaurant for first-class passengers, and the Café Parisien (see page 174), there were also first, second- and third-class dining saloons with a choice of courses within a set menu, and of course full bar and cellar facilities. The staff, both waiters and cooks, servicing the restaurants was vast in number, and it is sad to relate that virtually all of them died in the wreck. The A La Carte Restaurant was independently run more or less exclusively by French and Italian staff. The cooks were aided in their labours by a large number of new electrical devices, from potato-peelers to loaf-slicers, toasters and egg-boilers. There were pulverizing machines and bacon-slicers. Even bread produced on board was worked by electric kneaders. And roast meat, once an unheard-of luxury on ships, was turned out perfectly thanks to the Henry Wilson electric roasting ovens. Lamb, duck, beef and pork presented no problem, and fish and shellfish were equally plentiful. Of course, it was all prepared on a very grand scale: 10,000 covers a day wasn't unusual on a big liner, and Edwardians ate lunches and dinners that ran to several courses. Then there was the food laid in to cater for special diets, such as kosher and vegetarian, and for certain European preferences, such as knackwurst or mettwurst for Germans, or frogs' legs and snails for the French. On *Olympic*'s winter crossings the kitchen staff would have to lay in perhaps a ton of Christmas puddings and half a ton of mincemeat, and God knows how much turkey. The logistics of feeding so many disparate people, even if it were only for five or six days on the transatlantic crossing, must have been alarming.

Titanic's first- and second-class galley, opulently appointed, was situated on D deck, along with its butcher's shop, baker's shop, sculleries and pantries. It occupied a vast area, its pantries alone measuring 160 × 92 feet. The island range in the centre was 26 × 8 feet, with bains-marie and hot closets at each end, as well as a second single-fronted range 28¾ feet in length. The main first- and second-class pantries where the food was prepared for service were equipped in the most modern style, with steam-heated carving tables, entrée-presses (hot presses for entrées), hot-presses (for general use), coffee and hot-water boilers, automatic egg-boilers, bains-marie and electric hotplates. In the pantries there was enough space for one hundred waiters to move about freely, and the principal galley catered not only to first and second class, but to the officers' mess, the engineers' mess, the maids' and valets' saloon, and the Marconi operators' and postal clerks' mess. These were connected by dumb waiters, and another hoist was connected to the A La Carte Restaurant galley on B deck. There were also pantries to serve the first-class smoking room and the first-class lounge. The third-class galley was situated on the starboard side of F deck, and was a modest kitchen, taking up no more room than two first-class staterooms. Here, plain food in large quantities was prepared and served. There was a range, an oven, and four 80-gallon steam-cooking boilers.

The following facilities were available on *Olympic*, listed here in some detail and by deck (according to Bruce Beveridge). We may assume that *Titanic* was similarly equipped.

BOAT DECK
Officers' smoking room pantry
- I steam water-boiler, 4-gallon capacity
- I earthenware filter, 4-gallon capacity

Officers' mess room pantry
- I hot-press, 4 x 2¼ feet
- I steam water-boiler, 4-gallon capacity
- I earthenware filter, 4-gallon capacity

A DECK
First-class lounge and deck pantry
- I hot-press, 6 x 2½ feet

- I bain-marie, 3 x 2½ feet
- I set of coffee-makers, each having a 3-gallon capacity
- 2 patent cork-pullers (in lounge bar vestibule)
- I water-cooler, 20-gallon capacity

First-class smoking room pantry

- 2 electric hotplates, 12 inches in diameter, 850 watts each
- I electric coffee percolator, 4-gallon capacity, 2,400 watts
- I patent cork-puller
- I pressure filter, 8-gallon capacity
- I water-cooler, 20-gallon capacity

Forward stateroom pantry

- I steam water-boiler, 4-gallon capacity
- I pressure filter, 8-gallon capacity

B DECK

Restaurant

- 4 rechaud (reheating) stands

A La Carte Restaurant and galley

- I range 22¼ x 3 feet x 2 feet 10 inches with five ovens, 20½ feet x 26 inches x 18 inches with three fires and pan-rack over I bain-marie 2½ feet square with hot closet under, 27 cubic inches
- 2 portable bains-marie
- I hand-driven knife cleaner
- 2 electric toast 'salamanders'

- I electric triturator (grinding machine) with a 0.5 bhp motor
- I single grill 6¼ x 3 x 3 feet, with a hot closet over
- I hot press, 8¼ x 3 feet
- I electric soup machine
- 3 electric griddle cookers
- 3 American egg-boilers
- I steam water-boiler
- I mortar
- I steam oven
- I set of coffee-boilers, 3-gallon capacity each
- I patent cork-puller
- I water cooler, 20-gallon capacity
- 4 pressure filters, 6-gallon capacity

Second-class smoking room bar

- I electric hotplate, 12 inches diameter, 850 watts
- I coffee kettle
- I patent cork-puller
- I pressure filter, 8-gallon capacity

Two stateroom pantries (forward and midships)

- I steam water-boiler in each pantry, 4-gallon capacity
- I pressure filter, 8-gallon capacity (forward pantry only)

C DECK
Crew's galley

- I range 10 x 3 feet with three ovens and two fires
- I double wet-steam oven

- 3 steam-cooking boilers, 80-gallon capacity each
- 1 Cornhill brand potato-peeler and motor

Maids' and valets' pantry
- 1 hot press
- 1 set coffee-boilers
- 1 water-cooler

Third-class smoking room bar
- 1 patent cork-puller
- 1 pressure filter

Two stateroom pantries
- As on B deck

D DECK
Third-class bar
- 1 patent cork-puller

First-class forward entry foyer
- 2 hotplates, 12 inches diameter

First-class dining saloon pantry
- 2 hot-presses and carving tables, 14 x 2½ feet, bain-marie between
- 2 hotplates and cutting tables, bain-marie between
- 2 hotplates for soup
- 2 hotplates for vegetables
- 1 electric coffee mill
- 6 electric griddle cookers, each 2,500 watts
- 12 American egg-boilers
- 2 sets of coffee-boilers

- 2 milk-boilers
- 1 ice-crushing machine
- 2 patent cork-pullers
- 2 electric knife-cleaning machines

First- and second-class pantry

- 1 island range, 26 x 8 x 2 feet 10 inches, comprising 12 ovens, 8 fires, canopy, pan-racks and bain-marie
- 1 single-front range
- 7 ovens with accoutrements
- 2 hotplates
- 2 water steam cookers
- 1 double roaster
- 1 single roaster
- 2 double grills
- 6 steam stockpots
- 2 clean steam producers
- 1 electric soup machine
- 1 beef press
- 1 pestle and mortar (of industrial size)
- 2 portable ham-boilers
- 1 electric triturator

Bake house

- 1 Perkins oven
- 1 Phillips water-tube oven
- 1 range
- 1 baker's oven

First- and second-class baker's shop
- 2 bread provers
- 1 large electric dough mixer (supplied by W. H. Allen)
- 2 electric sorbet freezers
- 1 electric whisk
- 1 roll divider

First- and second-class butcher's shop
- 1 electric bacon slicer

Second-class dining saloon pantry
- 2 hot presses and carving tables, bain-marie
- 1 hot press for coffee cups
- 1 coffee mill
- 3 electric griddle cookers, 2,500 watts each
- 9 American egg-boilers
- 2 sets of coffee-boilers, 3-gallon capacity each
- 2 milk-boilers
- 1 cork-puller (in second-class saloon bar)
- 2 electric knife-cleaning machines (in second-class knife room)
- 1 water cooler

First-class stateroom pantry (forward)
- 1 steam water-boiler
- 1 pressure filter

E DECK

First-class stateroom pantry (midships)
- 1 steam water-boiler

Engineers' mess room pantry
- 1 hot-press

- 1 steam water-boiler

Potato wash place

- 1 electric potato-peeler, 0.75 bhp motor

F DECK

Third-class dining saloon pantries

- 4 hot-presses
- 2 sets of coffee-boilers
- 2 water-boilers

Third-class galley

- 1 range
- 2 baker's ovens
- 1 double wet-steam oven
- 4 steam-cooking boilers, 80-gallon capacity each

Third-class bakery

- 1 ordinary-size electric dough maker
- 1 bread prover

Third-class potato wash place

- 1 electric potato-peeler, 0.75 bhp motor

And to complement all this equipment there was an impressive array of cutlery, crockery and glassware. *Titanic* carried about 21,000 pieces of cutlery, plus napkin-rings and 3,000 metal dishes and tureens, supplied by Elkington's of Birmingham. On *Olympic* the items included the following (and we may assume similar, if not greater quantities, on *Titanic*).

- 400 sugar basins
- 400 fruit dishes
- 1,000 finger bowls
- 400 butter dishes
- 400 vegetable dishes
- 8,000 dinner forks
- 1,500 fruit forks
- 1,500 fish forks
- 1,000 oyster forks
- 400 cream jugs
- 400 butter knives
- 1,500 fruit knives
- 1,500 fish knives
- 8,000 table and dessert knives
- 400 nutcrackers
- 400 toast-racks
- 5,000 dinner spoons
- 3,000 dessert spoons
- 1,500 mustard spoons
- 100 grape scissors
- 400 asparagus tongs
- 400 sugar tongs

As for crockery, in first class it was bone china, often edged with 22-carat gold leaf. Other crockery included:

- 4,500 breakfast cups
- 3,000 teacups
- 1,500 coffee cups
- 3,000 beef-tea cups (Bovril was a very popular drink in those days)
- 1,000 cream jugs
- 2,500 breakfast plates
- 2,000 dessert plates
- 12,000 dinner plates
- 4,500 soup dishes
- 1,200 coffee pots
- 1,200 teapots
- 4,500 breakfast saucers
- 3,000 tea saucers
- 1,200 pie dishes
- 1,000 meat dishes

In addition to all this, Royal Crown Derby, which supplied the crockery for the A La Carte Restaurant, delivered a set of dinnerware to Harland & Wolff in December 1911 (no doubt destined for *Titanic*'s A La Carte Restaurant) consisting of 600 dinner plates, 180 soup dishes, 180 breakfast plates, 100 salad plates, 100 breakfast cups and saucers, 100 teacups and saucers, 25 cream jugs and 25 slop-basins. Stonier's, the Liverpool supplier of Royal Crown Derby to the White Star Line, tried to drive a hard bargain with Crown Derby, arguing that the publicity the company would receive justified a lower price. Crown Derby's own publicity blurb was along these lines:

A design in exquisite taste has been chosen for the china for the 'Titanic', consisting of a band of encrusted gold work with painted ornament of Chaplets and Festoons in the Louis XVI style, delicately finished in tints of green. Each article bears the monogram of the Oceanic Steam Navigation Company (White Star Line) in similar colouring, and the whole effect is very chaste. Travellers who take their meals in the Restaurant of the 'Titanic' will have their viands served on china entirely superior to that provided at any of the finest hotels in the Kingdom. Too little attention has, in the past, been paid to matters of this kind, and the White Star Company are to be congratulated on their new departure, which will doubtless be immensely appreciated by their patrons. The arrangements for the supply of the China have been made by Messrs. Stonier & Co. of 78 Lord Street, Liverpool, who have for many years supplied the whole of the Table, Glass and China appointments of the magnificent White Star Fleet.

A good deal of the crockery used by White Star was made in the Potteries around Stoke-on-Trent. Decorating crockery was a highly sought-after occupation for Edwardian working-class women, who made up 60 per cent of the pottery factory workers. Most of *Titanic's* china was painstakingly gilded and painted in Staffordshire factories, but the workers were paid piece-work rates and had to complete four plates an hour; what's more, they were penalized for any mistakes. Although in general the pottery companies were good employers, building houses for their employees and running choirs for their edification, there was no redress in the event of injury, or of illness deriving from the inhalation of pottery dust and lead glazes, known as pneumoconiosis.

Identifying the problems women workers faced if injury precluded them from work, the wonderful Millicent Fanny St Clair Erskine, later Leverson-Gower, Duchess of Sutherland (1867–1955) – a thrice-married (and twice-divorced) society hostess, author, editor, playwright and journalist (her nom de plume was Erskine Gower), and also a leading social reformer – set up her own factory to employ them, and ran it at a profit, to the annoyance of other factory owners, who called her 'Meddlesome Millie', a nickname she was proud of. She mentioned it in a speech reported in the *New York Times* on 7 July 1912, and went on to say: 'The day is coming when no-one will be grateful for the crumbs that fall from the rich man's table. It will be a good day too. We absolutely must advance, and if there is some squealing about the advance and a little overhurry about it, at any rate people can see the break at the end of the tunnel and know they will emerge into fuller light.' And I can't resist telling you that Millie was awarded the Croix de Guerre for her Red Cross work during the Great War. What a woman!

Cutlery in first class was Sheffield silver plate with fluted handles, and the glassware was by Stuart Crystal of Stourbridge. That in second class was predictably more middle class, and that in third class was purely functional. Glassware on *Olympic* (etched with the White Star logo) comprised:

- 8,000 cut-glass tumblers
- 2,500 water-bottles
- 1,500 crystal dishes
- 300 celery glasses
- 500 flower vases
- 5,500 ice-cream dishes
- 2,000 wine glasses
- 2,500 champagne glasses
- 1,500 cocktail glasses
- 1,200 liqueur glasses
- 300 claret jugs
- 2,000 salt-cellars
- 500 salad bowls
- 1,500 soufflé dishes
- 1,200 pudding bowls

Crown Derby wasn't the only supplier of crockery. Bisto, Brownfield's, Copeland, Foley, Minton, Samson & Bridgwood and Spode also supplied White Star liners.

There was no design exclusive to *Titanic*, though different designs were used in different classes, dining rooms, cafés and saloons. The first-class dining saloon, for example, had plates, often with scalloped edges, that might feature a brown and turquoise border, and each piece carried the White Star Line logo in its centre. In second class, Delftware was widely used on the Olympic-class ships; in third, crockery was plain white but still bore the White Star logo – a red pennant with a white star – at the centre of plates.

Special facilities were also available for observant Jews. Not only were their culinary requirements respected, but they were provided with their own crockery, marked MEAT and MILK, for example, in Hebrew and English. *Titanic* carried one kosher chef. (Apparently no special arrangements were made for Muslims because they were not frequent travellers a hundred years ago.)

The theft of items as souvenirs was often a problem, and may have been one reason why White Star didn't have the name of a particular ship on its crockery or glassware. Nevertheless, things such as ashtrays and tea towels were routinely purloined. Beveridge even cites an instance of an officer's uniform buttons being cut off a jacket left on a hanger in his unlocked cabin during his absence.

FOOD SUPPLIES

Notwithstanding that the Olympic-class liners were effectively American ships, food supplies were regulated by the British Board of Trade. Quantities were determined by the size and capacity of the ship (crew and passengers), as well as by speed, number of propellers, and duration of voyage. Allowance was made for additional time at sea occasioned by, for example, breakdown (a single-screw steamer would be at a total loss if disabled, so such a ship had to be provisioned for at least twenty-six days). In fact, the travel ticket (which was also a form of contract) issued to passengers carried a list of provisions statutorily provided. What follows comes from a third-class White Star ticket of 1910:

The following quantities, at least, of Water and Provisions will be supplied by the Master (captain) of the ship, as required by law, viz.:

To each statute adult (a statute adult may also be deemed to constitute more than one child below a certain age), 4 quarts of water daily, exclusive of what is required for cooking the articles required by the Merchant Shipping Act, 1908, to be issued in a cooked state and a weekly allowance of provisions according to the following scale:- 2.25 pounds Beef or Pork, or partly one and partly the other, 1 pound Preserved Meat, 6 ounces Suet, 4 ounces Butter, 2.25 pounds Bread or Biscuit (not inferior in quality to Navy Biscuit), 3.5 pounds Wheaton Flour (not inferior to best seconds), 2 pounds Oatmeal, Rice and Peas, or any two of them, 2 pounds Potatoes, 6 ounces Raisins, 2 ounces Tea, 1 pound Sugar, 2 ounces Salt, 0.5 ounce Mustard, 0.25 ounce Black or White Pepper, ground, 8 ounces Dried or Compressed Vegetables, 1 gill Vinegar or Mixed Pickles.

For children between one and four years of age, in addition to half-rations of the above-named articles:- 3 gills Preserved Milk, 10 ounces Condensed Egg, or 3 ounces Fresh Eggs. For children between four and twelve months of age:- 21 pints Water, 7 gills Preserved Milk, 9 ounces Preserved Soup, 10 ounces Condensed Egg, or 3 ounces Fresh Eggs, 12 ounces Biscuit, 4 ounces Oatmeal, 8 ounces Flour, 4 ounces Rice, 10 ounces Sugar.

Substitution of the following rates may, at the option of the Master of any 'Passenger Ship', be made in the above dietary scale, that is to say:- 1.5 pounds Fresh Meat, 1 pound Salt Meat, 0.75 pound Preserved Meat to be considered equal. 0.5 ounce Coffee, 0.25 ounce Cocoa, 0.25 ounce Tea to be considered equal. 1 pint Split Peas, 0.75 pound Flour, 0.5 pint Calavances [a kind of pulse] or Haricot Beans, 0.75 pound Rice to be considered equal when issued with Meat rations. 1 pound Marmalade, 1 pound Jam, 0.5 pound Butter to be considered equal. Mustard and Curry powder to be considered equal.

Again, the business of ordering, delivering and storing the vast quantities of food and drink called for very sophisticated logistics, especially as foodstuffs were garnered from around the world – fruit from California, cheese from France, oysters from Baltimore, ice cream from New York, coffee from Brazil, tea from India, lamb from Berkshire, and so on. For the transatlantic voyage, *Olympic* and doubtless *Titanic* too laid on the following stores:

Fresh meats, 75,000 pounds; fresh fish, 11,000 pounds; salt- and dried fish, 4,000 pounds; bacon and ham, 7,500 pounds; poultry and game, 8,000 head; fresh butter, 6,000 pounds; fresh eggs, 40,000; sausages, 2,500 pounds; sweetbreads, 1,000; ice cream, 1,750 quarts; coffee, 2,200 pounds; tea, 800 pounds; peas, rice & co., 10,000 pounds; sugar, 10,000 pounds; assorted jams, 1,120 pounds; flour, 200 barrels; potatoes, 40 tons; apples and oranges, 180 boxes each (36,000 pieces each); lemons, 50 boxes; grapefruit, 50 boxes; hothouse grapes, 1,000 pounds; fresh milk, 1,500 gallons; condensed milk, 600 gallons; cream, 1,000 quarts; fresh asparagus, 800 bundles; onions, 3,500 pounds; fresh green peas, 1.25 tons; tomatoes, 2.75 tons; beer and stout, 20,000 bottles; mineral water, 15,000 bottles; wine, 1,500 bottles; spirits, 800 bottles; cigars, 8,000.

No expense was spared for top-paying passengers, and as English produce in many cases was considered superior to American, grapes, nectarines and peaches, salmon, sole and turbot, beef, mutton and lamb were all shipped from Great Britain for use on the eastward passage back. All perishable foodstuffs were subject to inspection, and food left over but still usable at the end of a voyage was sealed in cold compartments. Food for crew consumption between voyages (had she survived, *Titanic* would have made her eastward return trip on 20 April) was strictly monitored.

THE A LA CARTE RESTAURANT AND THE DINING SALOONS

As for dining facilities, each class had its own saloon. In first class, tables were arranged as in a normal restaurant to seat two people each and groups of four, six, eight and even ten. There was a twelve-seater table as well in the middle of the first-class dining saloon. On *Titanic*, Captain Smith favoured a six-seater because the smaller number made conversation easier. In second and third class there were long tables with seating either side – traditional shipboard dining arrangements.

In first class there was one waiter to every three diners. Breakfast was served 8.00–10.00 a.m., lunch from 1.00 p.m., tea from 4.00 p.m. and dinner from 7.00 p.m., these times varying slightly according to the direction of the voyage. A first-class passenger giving advance notice to the second steward no later than 1.30 p.m. could arrange to dine later in the first-class saloon. The A La Carte Restaurant, available only to first-class passengers, was open all day, but the cost of meals here wasn't included in the ticket price. Passengers opting for the A La Carte Restaurant got a rebate of £5 on their ticket, but they had to forgo the use of the first-class dining saloon. Dining à la carte started at 12s 6d (62½ pence) per head, without wine – a lot of money a hundred years ago.

A la carte restaurants were frowned upon by some traditionalists when they were first introduced on ships, but they were an instant hit with rich passengers, and they carried a good deal of cachet and snob value. Their introduction suited the shipping lines too because they provided an economical way of catering for people who didn't care to take their meals at fixed hours. On *Titanic* this restaurant opened at 8.00 a.m. and served continuously until 11.00 p.m. Its appeal lay not only in its flexible hours, but in its flexible menu, as saloon meals were truly Edwardian in the number of courses and the heaviness of the dishes. And if the dining saloon should happen to be overbooked, White Star could offer special deals to passengers in order to entice them to use the A La Carte. A typical menu might include roast chicken, roast duck, roast squab, chicken Maryland or Lyonnaise, beef, pork or lamb, mutton chops (a popular breakfast dish), lobster, oysters, turbot, as well as asparagus and all manner of vegetables. Desserts included Waldorf pudding, lemon meringue pie and apple crumble. And the wine list was exemplary.

The last dinner served on board *Titanic* (first-class saloon) is worth noting in proper detail, as it would have been served. And it is worth bearing in mind that half an hour after retiring following this meal (shown overleaf), first-class passengers were expected to rouse themselves and head for the lifeboats. No wonder many of them were reluctant to do so.

'I remember that last meal on the *Titanic* very well. We had a big vase of beautiful daffodils on the table, which were as fresh as if they had just been picked.'
Lady Duff Gordon, *Discretions and Indiscretions*, 1932

FIRST COURSE/
HORS D'OEUVRES
Canapés à l'amiral
Huitres à la Russe
(White Bordeaux, Burgundy
or Chablis)
—
SOUP
Consommé Olga
Cream of barley
(Madeira or Sherry)
—
FISH
Poached salmon with sauce
mousseline
(Rhine, Moselle)
—
ENTRÉES
Filet mignon Lili
Sauté of chicken Lyonnaise
Vegetable marrow farcie
(Red Bordeaux)
—
REMOVES
Lamb with mint sauce
Calvados-glazed roast
duckling with apple sauce
Roast sirloin of beef forestière
Château potatoes
Minted green pea timbales
Creamed carrots
Steamed rice
Parmentier and boiled
new potatoes
(Red Burgundy or Beaujolais)

PUNCH/SORBET
Punch romaine
—
ROAST
Roasted squab on wilted cress
(Red Burgundy)
—
SALAD
Cold asparagus salad with
champagne-saffron vinaigrette
—
COLD DISH
Pâté de foie gras with celery
(Sauternes or sweet Rhine)
—
PUDDING
Waldorf pudding
Peaches in Chartreuse jelly
Chocolate-painted éclairs with
French vanilla ice cream
French vanilla ice cream
(Muscatel, Tokay, Sauternes)
—
DESSERT
Assorted fresh fruit and cheeses
(Dessert wine, prosecco, cava,
champagne)
—
TO END
Coffee, liqueurs, port, cognac,
armagnac
Cigars
Cordials

Passengers in first class were expected to wear black tie for dinner, though not necessarily on the days of embarkation and disembarkation. The dinner hour was announced by the ship's bugler, who would sound either 'Come To The Cookhouse Door' or, more usually, 'The Roast Beef Of Old England', and he would sound a dressing call half an hour before that. Passengers signed for drinks much as they do today on cruise ships, and settled up with their table or room steward at the end of the trip.

The elegant reception room at the forward end of the first-class dining saloon was a place to meet and have a martini before dinner, or to linger over coffee and cognac afterwards. *Shipbuilder* magazine described it: '. . . friends and parties will meet [here] prior to taking their seats in the restaurant. The elegant settees and easy chairs are upholstered in silk of carmine colour, with embroideries applied in tasteful design. The breadth of treatment and the carefully proportioned panels on the walls, with richly carved cornice and surrounding mouldings, form an impressive *ensemble*, which is distinctly pleasing to the eye. There is accommodation for a band in this room.' The A La Carte Restaurant also had a small reception room attached to it. Smoking was allowed here at all times, and the band played between 8.00 and 9.15 in the evening.

Second-class passengers were summoned to dine by a gong, and though clearly their fare was not as lavish as that provided in first class, the food was good and more than adequate. Luncheon might consist of pea soup, spaghetti au gratin, corned beef or roast mutton; and for dinner the second-class diner might get haddock, chicken curry or roast turkey. There could be two sittings for breakfast, lunch and dinner, which tended to take pressure off the staff in the combined first- and second-class galley. The third-class saloon was placed midships, and although it was plain in decor and style, it was still well above the average for such a shipboard dining room. Mealtimes were staggered here as well, and the room itself was divided in two by watertight bulkhead H. Printed menus here doubled as postcards, which could either be mailed home ('free' advertising for White Star) or kept as souvenirs. Menus were prepared in advance for each meal for each day of the trip, whereas in first and second class, menus were presented individually. But there was nothing wrong with either the quality or the quantity of food offered to the humbler passengers.

CHAPTER TEN

LAYOUT

HAVING BEEN FITTED AND equipped as described in the previous chapters, *Titanic* was now complete and ready to sail (with a skeleton crew) from Belfast to Southampton. There she would take on the bulk of her passengers and crew and leave around lunchtime on Wednesday, 10 April for Cherbourg, Queenstown and (everyone believed) New York. But the fine details were by no means finished. Amid the ceaseless noise of hammering, Thomas Andrews, principal designer, stalked the ship, chasing workmen to complete the finishing touches as they sailed.

BOAT DECK

The Boat deck was the highest, and, thanks to the Sirocco ventilating fans, was not cluttered with the large ventilator cowls that on the *Mauretania* delivered air to the boiler-rooms. Decked in yellow pine, interrupted by the raised roofs of the first-class reading and writing room and lounge, the chief features here were the navigating bridge and the wheelhouse, both of which offered broad views of the sea 58 feet below. Here too were the lifeboats slung on their davits, but with an interruption midships where there were no boats, since they would spoil the views from the first-class promenade.

The navigating bridge, set back 198 feet from the stem, was 27 feet wide and stood 8 feet above deck level. Built of teak and pine, it ended on port and starboard with wing-cabs from which navigation in dock or harbour could be directed. The wheelhouse was directly behind and above the bridge, also made of wood, and forming the forward end of the officers' quarters' deckhouse.

Watches were run on the time-honoured principle of First, 8.00 p.m. until midnight; Second, midnight until 4.00 a.m.; Morning, 4.00 a.m. until 8.00 a.m.; Forenoon, 8.00 a.m.until midday; Afternoon, midday until 4.00 p.m., followed by the two Dogwatches, 4.00 p.m. until 6.00 p.m. and 6.00 p.m. until 8.00 p.m., incorporated to break the four-hour pattern, thus ensuring that no one stood the same hours repeatedly. (Dogwatch, by the way, derives from Sirius, the Dog Star, the first to appear at the beginning of these watches.)

The navigating room (primarily for the captain's use and with a forward-facing window) and chart room were next to the wheelhouse, within the officers' deckhouse itself. There was also a cabin for the pilot. Aft of the navigating room were the captain's rooms, which ran fore and aft on the starboard side close to Number 1 funnel and comprised a living room, bedroom and bathroom, and were connected to the navigating room just forward of the living room. Quarters for the chief, first, second, third and fifth officers were located on the port side, while the fourth officer was just aft of the captain's bathroom and just forward of the officers' smoking room. The Marconi operators' office and quarters were just aft of that again, in the middle of the ship, with no porthole or natural daylight. Their wireless aerials were attached to the roof of the deckhouse above to the overhead wires between the masts.

On *Titanic* there were six (modest) first-class staterooms aft of the officers' quarters, and aft again of them was the first-class grand staircase dome and the first-class entrance lobby. Near this, on the starboard side, was the gymnasium (available to first-class passengers only). This spacious area contained two cycling machines (with a great dial for measuring speed and distance so that you could have 'races'), two 'horses', one 'camel' and two rowing-machines, as well as weights, massagers for back and front, and a punch-ball. The electrically powered exercisers were supplied by Rossel, Schwarz of Wiesbaden.

Deck games were played on this level, and the officers' mess, served by a dumb waiter from the first-class pantry on D deck, was also located here.

The gymnasium was open to men from 6.00 a.m. to 9.00 a.m., and to ladies from 10.00 a.m. until 1.00 p.m. Children were permitted from then until 3.00 p.m., and men again from 4.00 p.m. until 6.00 p.m. There was a fully qualified instructor, T. W. McCawley, who sadly went down with the ship, as did Lt-Colonel John Jacob Astor IV, the millionaire builder, hotelier, inventor, property developer and writer, who on the day of the wreck waited in the gymnasium until the lifeboats were ready.

SCANDAL AND SADNESS

John Jacob Astor had taken fairly modest first-class accommodation (which nevertheless cost about £224) on *Titanic* in order not to attract too much attention. He was travelling with his new wife, Madeleine, thirty years his junior (he was forty-seven, she eighteen), and there was an aura of post-divorce scandal. Astor was the richest passenger aboard – richer than Isidor Straus, owner of Macy's department store, and richer than Benjamin Guggenheim, both of whom also went down with the ship, though Straus's age and Guggenheim's public standing would have guaranteed them places in lifeboats.

Astor conducted his already-pregnant wife, her maid and nurse to Boat 4 at 1.55 a.m. on Monday, 15 April. He wanted to accompany them, but when Second Officer Charles Lightoller told him that men couldn't board until all women and children had been looked after, he accepted without complaint and just handed his wife his gloves to keep her hands warm. He moved to a position near Number 1 funnel and was crushed by it when it fell. His battered body was recovered by *CS Mackay-Bennett* on 22 April.

A DECK

Also known as the Promenade deck, A deck was the next below the Boat deck, and at 546 feet long, it extended the entire length of the superstructure. This deck was exclusive to first-class passengers, and was in effect their main exercise deck, partly protected from the weather, and housing a number of principal staterooms as well as public rooms. The lounge and its pantry were located just aft of Number 3 funnel, and it was on this deck that Thomas Andrews had his cabin (A36 port). Father Francis Browne (an interesting character, described in more detail in Chapter 11) had A37 starboard; and the Duff-Gordons were in A20 port (south if travelling west). These were relatively modest first-class staterooms, though Andrews did have a bathroom immediately next door. Staterooms A3 and A4 were the largest and best on this deck.

The first-class, so-called 'grand' staircases in William and Mary style were the great showpieces on both *Olympic* and *Titanic* (and would have been on *Britannic* too had it not been for the First World War). They would have graced any Edwardian stately home of the nouveaux riches. The forward staircase was placed between Numbers 1 and 2 funnels, and led from A down to F deck. The Boat deck and A deck entrances were topped by the elegant glass dome already described, and the space it encompassed allowed it to branch into a double tier. Where the forward staircase debouched on to A deck, its central partition was decked with a large bronze cherub holding an (electric) torch.

A deck also held the first-class reading and writing

room, aft of Number 2 funnel, intended for the use of ladies (men had the smoking room, which to the modern eye looks very like an elegant public-house saloon of about 1900). Aft of this was the first-class lounge, a magnificent salon, pronounced by many persons the finest room ever built into a ship. It was a vast and light room, panelled in the very best English oak, featuring an 18-foot bookcase, a 5-foot fireplace, an ormolu electrolier, and a white and gilt plasterwork ceiling. Here one could take tea and coffee between 8.00 a.m. and 11.30 p.m., and borrow books from the massive bookcase via the room steward.

Also on this deck were the first-class veranda and palm courts, airy cafés decorated loosely in the Louis XVI style.

B DECK
The top weight-bearing deck, and 555 feet long, B deck was where most first-class accommodation was to be found. This included the two palatial midships parlour suites (B52, 54 and 56 port, and B51, 53 and 55 starboard) with their private enclosed promenades on either side of Number 2 funnel. By contrast, staterooms B4 and B3, right forward and port and starboard respectively, were the most modest first-class rooms, though they were in a prime location with brilliant views forward. All staterooms had a Prometheus electric heater in a shelved case, a ceiling fan, luggage racks where possible, lamps, wardrobes, wash-basins and clothes hooks.

B deck was also the home of the A La Carte

Restaurant. This was situated between the turbine engine casing and the forward second-class companionway, and comprised 50 tables seating 140 diners. Its decor was (heavy Edwardian) Louis XVI. It had its own pantry and galley, and was run on a subcontracted basis by the thirty-six-year-old London-Italian immigrant Luigi Gatti of Oddenino's, the Ritz Adelphi and the Ritz Strand of London, and his staff. They even ran to supplying diners with corsages and boutonnières from the Southampton firm of Bealing's. Gatti's body was recovered by the SS *Minia*, his corpse numbered 313, and his effects listed as one gold watch and chain, one sovereign case, one Kruger sovereign, one silver matchbox, $6 in notes, monogrammed 'LG' cufflinks, one diamond ring, two collar buttons, one knife marked 'Imperial restaurant', one key, one eraser, one lead pencil, 7 sovereigns in a case, 2 half-sovereigns, 5s 6d in silver, assorted copper coins, one bunch of keys with tags ('comptroller's office restaurant 1st class entrance B deck' and 'restaurant manager, entrance to Café Parisien'), laundry marked on linen collar 'HR', two pocket knives marked 'HR', and one pair of gloves. Gatti left an English wife, Edith, and a son, Vittorio.

Another casualty was one of the chefs in the A La Carte Restaurant, a Frenchman called Pierre Rousseau. A former employee of Luigi Gatti, Rousseau had signed on for the voyage on 6 April 1912. At forty-nine, he had been working in Britain for some time, at the North British Station Hotel in Edinburgh, and latterly at one of Gatti's London establishments. On the night of the wreck he made it to the deck with his friend and compatriot, kitchen clerk Paul Mauge. Mauge jumped into a lifeboat and beckoned Rousseau to follow, but Rousseau demurred, saying that he was too fat, and if he jumped, he might overset or even smash the lifeboat. So he stayed aboard. His body was never recovered.

On the starboard side of the restaurant was the Café Parisien, long, narrow and light, with 21 tables seating 68 people. Its particular appeal was to rich Americans who were smitten with Paris.

B deck was also the site of the second-class entrance hall and smoking room, the latter very similar, though more modest, in style to that of first class, with leather-bound tub seats grouped around square tables. This deck also held some second-class cabins, accessed by the second-class lift that ascended to this level. A covered promenade for second-class passengers ran on port and starboard sides. Right forward on this level was the Forecastle deck, bearing Number 1 hatch, four capstans, two windlasses and the central anchor housing. It was reserved for professional use, so the scenes here in the 1997 film *Titanic* lack authenticity. Astern was the Poop deck, which comprised a third-class promenade, as well as four capstans and two electric cranes. Also here was the docking bridge, used for guiding the ship into harbour.

C DECK

Also known as the Shelter deck, C deck was the highest level to run without interruption from stem to stern. The forward Well deck was situated just aft of the Forecastle deck, where there was another promenade for third class, and forward of this ran a range of staterooms, both first and second class, as well as the enquiry office and the adjacent purser's office (near the grand staircase). There were more suites here, though without promenades, one of which (in Regency style) was occupied by Isidor and Ida Straus of Macy's department store, New York, who did not survive the sinking. 'What a ship!' wrote Mrs Straus to a friend on 10 April. 'So huge and magnificently appointed. Our rooms are furnished in the best of taste and most luxuriously, and they are really rooms, not cabins.' There were second-class staterooms and superior crew accommodation here too, plus the second-class library (which doubled as the lounge), near the doctors' accommodation and surgery aft. The surgery led via a staircase to the hospital on D deck, where there was also a surgery for third-class passengers.

On the port side was the first-class barber's shop. Here too, well forward, were the messes of seamen, firemen and greasers, the crew's galley and their surgery.

The after Well deck housed more professional equipment, as well as the third-class bar, smoking room and general room – a plain, but light, airy and spacious room, having pictures, a wall-clock and potted plants. (Raymond Bealing, whose grandfather's firm supplied the floral decorations and pot plants to White Star, told Southampton City Heritage Oral History: 'If the plant locations were similar to those on her [*Titanic's*] sister ship the SS [*sic*] *Olympic*, then perhaps some 300 to 400 plants in 5-inch pots would have been required . . . I think that in those days small plants were used as decoration on the restaurant tables.')

D DECK

Descending again, D deck forward furnished accommodation for 108 firemen in two dormitories, port and starboard, of fifty-four beds each, each fifty-four corresponding to a watch. And D deck was also the first in order of descent to carry berths for seamen, greasers and trimmers as well. Aft of these arrangements were more first-class staterooms, and towards the stern were a number of second-class staterooms. Just aft of midships were the first- and second-class combined galley with its pantries, and the huge first- and second-class dining saloons (respectively fore and aft of the galley) with their fiddled tables (the fiddle being a raisable rim for use in rough weather to prevent things sliding to the floor). The second-class saloon seated 394 diners and was 71 feet long overall. Later in her career, by the way, *Olympic*'s long tables in second class were replaced by smaller ones, as in a conventional restaurant, adapting to the growing taste for more privacy.

Aftermost on D deck were third-class cabins. These, like all after third-class rooms, were for single women and families – single men being berthed forward. Latrines were located here, as were the only two bathrooms available to the humbler passenger.

E DECK

Also known as Upper deck, E deck was the highest continuous deck to which all the watertight bulkheads rose, though eight of the fifteen (C–J) went up as far as the deck above. E deck was principally given over to accommodation for crew and passengers alike, crew mainly forward, though there were a few third-class staterooms towards the stem as well. A long, broad corridor, nicknamed Scotland Road (after a famous Liverpool thoroughfare, though it was known as Bond Street to the officers), ran along this deck for professional use, and the engineers' mess and the stewards, stewardesses, and restaurant staff were mainly quartered here. This was the lowest deck to which the first-class lifts ran because there were still first-class staterooms amidships, giving way to second and then third class as you moved aft. The musicians and the purser's clerks berthed here, and it was also the location of the second-class barber's shop, fitted, as in first class, with two Koken patent revolving chairs on oak frames.

F DECK

Also known as Middle deck, this level was principally fitted for third-class staterooms (though there was second-class accommodation here too) and crew accommodation (including the chief engineer's suite, which was very well appointed, as befitted his standing on the ship). Also housed here were the postal workers. On this level too were the third-class dining saloon, galley and pantry, plus the squash court gallery, the swimming pool – a great novelty – the Turkish bath with its attendant steam and massage rooms, and its electric bath. This last device resembled an iron lung: you would lie down in it with your head sticking out, and electric lights on the inside would warm your body. *Olympic* was fitted with two, but *Titanic* had only one.

G DECK

Also known as Lower deck, this level was the last that carried passengers and the last with portholes. Its length was broken up by boiler and engine casings, and its rooms were for third-class passengers and crew, though some of them had superior fittings in case they needed to be used as second-class staterooms. A few had removable berths and bulkheads so they could be adapted for storage. There were also compartments on this level for a variety of food, from poultry to ice cream. The squash court (another novelty) was located here, as was the post office.

ORLOP DECKS AND TANK TOP

Towards the bottom of *Titanic* we come to the Orlop decks and the Tank top. Here were the holds, the mail-room and the specie room (see page 137), as well as the machinery that drove the vessel. Motor cars in transit were crated up here, and there were refrigerated rooms for anything from champagne to fresh flowers.

And here this tour ends. It now remains to people the ship with crew and passengers.

CHAPTER ELEVEN

CREW AND PASSENGERS

MARCH 1912 SAW FAIRLY frantic activity on *Titanic* as the last touches were made to her fitting out. She was due to sail from Belfast to Southampton – a voyage of some 570 miles – on 1 April, but strong winds that day meant that both her sea trials and her departure were delayed by 24 hours. Staffed by her officers and a skeleton crew, together with Thomas Andrews and his 'guarantee crew' of craftsmen and fitters who were there to iron out any snags, and Harold Sanderson, a director of White Star, she was towed out of her deepwater wharf by four Liverpool tugs and into Belfast Lough for her sea trials. During these the engines were tested, the compasses adjusted, and trial transmissions made by the Marconi wireless men. The Board of Trade inspector, Francis Carruthers, signed and dated the ship's certificate as 'good for one year from today, 2.4.12', and Andrews and Sanderson signed the acceptance papers for White Star. Andrews also dropped a quick line to his wife: '. . . to let you know that we got away this morning in fine style and have had a very satisfactory trial. We are getting more ship-shape every hour, but there is still a great deal to be done.'

Titanic left Belfast about 8.00 p.m., arriving at 44 Berth in Southampton docks late the following day. On Thursday, 4 April Andrews wrote again to his wife: 'I wired you this morning of our safe arrival after a very satisfactory trip. The weather was good and everyone most pleasant. I think the ship will clean up all right before sailing on Wednesday.'

'The new Royal Mail triple-screw steamer *Titanic*, which has been built by Harland & Wolff Ltd, for the White Star Line, left the deepwater wharf shortly after 10 o'clock yesterday morning for Southampton, whence she will sail on her maiden voyage to New York on the 10th inst. The usual scenes of bustle and animation attending the departure of a great liner were witnessed from an early hour in the morning, and as the hawsers were cast off, the *Titanic* – the largest vessel in the world – floated proudly on the water, a monument to the enterprise of her owners and the ingenuity of the eminent firm who built her. She was at once taken in tow by the powerful tugs which were in attendance and the crowds of spectators who had assembled on both sides of the river raised hearty cheers as she was towed into the channel. The mammoth vessel presented an

> impressive spectacle, looking perfect from keel to truck, while the weather conditions were happily of favourable character. When the tugs were left behind the compasses were adjusted, after which a satisfactory speed run took place, and the latest triumph of the ship-builder's art then left for Southampton, carrying with her the best wishes of the citizens of Belfast.'
>
> *Belfast News Letter*, 3 April 1912

SIGNING ON THE CREW

The next job, and it had to be done quickly, was to sign up the rest of the crew. There was no such thing as a permanent crew in those days and there were also complications among the officers. Henry Wilde was brought on from *Olympic* as chief officer, which meant that the designated chief officer, William Murdoch, had to step down to the rank of first officer; Charles Lightoller then became second officer, and the original second officer, David Blair, was dropped from the complement altogether – to his bitter disappointment at the time, but later, of course, to his intense relief. Despite the impermanence of crews, there was still some continuity. For example, restaurant and cabin stewards often stayed in one ship for several voyages, but this wasn't true of other crew, and certainly not of stokers. About 40 per cent of the crew were Southampton natives, and 60 per cent were recruited in the town – indeed, Endle Street got the nickname 'Street of Tears' because so many men from it were lost in the wreck.

Of the crew, twenty-three were women – eighteen stewardesses, the third-class matron, Mrs Wallis, two masseuses and two cashiers employed in the first-class restaurant. Several were from Liverpool, following their employers south when White Star changed its port of departure in 1907. Three of the female crew, including Mrs Wallis, lost their lives in the wreck.

'Violet Constance Jessop (born 1 October 1887) worked on all three Olympic-class liners as a stewardess and nurse. She was the daughter of Irish emigrants living close to Bahía Blanca, Argentina, where her father had established himself as a sheep farmer. His fiancée, Katherine Kelly, followed him out there from Dublin in 1886. Violet was the first of nine children, only six of whom survived. Violet herself contracted TB at an early age, but survived despite gloomy prognostications from the doctors.

After the death of her father, Violet and her family moved to England, where she attended a convent school. At the age of twenty-three she took a job as a stewardess on *Olympic* and was on board when the ship's first major mishap occurred on 20 September 1911, as it collided with HMS *Hawke* off the Isle of Wight.

Violet joined *Titanic* as a stewardess on 10 April 1912. When disaster struck, she was ordered up on deck, where she watched as the crew loaded the boats. She herself was ordered into lifeboat 16, and as the boat was being lowered, one of *Titanic*'s officers gave her a baby to look after. The following morning Violet, and the rest of the survivors, were rescued by *Carpathia*. While she was on board the *Carpathia*, en route to New York, a woman grabbed the baby she was guarding and ran off with it without saying a word.

During the First World War, Violet served as a nurse for the British Red Cross, and in 1916 was aboard *Britannic*, which was doing service as a hospital ship. While in the Aegean, the ship struck a mine and went down. Violet, who had made it to a lifeboat, leapt out when she feared it being sucked into *Britannic*'s propellers – the cause of a number of fatalities. However, she was still sucked under water, and struck her head on the ship's keel, before being rescued by another lifeboat. She said later that the cushioning of her thick auburn hair had helped save her life. She'd also grabbed her toothbrush before leaving her cabin on *Britannic*, saying later that it was the one thing she missed most, following the wreck of *Titanic*.

After the war Violet continued to work for White Star, before joining the Red Star Line and then Royal Mail Ships. During her time with Red Star, she went on two world cruises on the company's largest ship, *Belgenland*.

In 1950 she retired to Suffolk. Many years later she got a telephone call from a woman claiming to be the

baby she saved from *Titanic*. Violet's friend and biographer John Maxtone-Graham said it was probably
someone playing a joke on her. She replied, 'I have never
told that story to anyone but you.' To this day, the baby
she saved has not been identified.

Violet Jessop died of heart failure on 5 May 1971 in
her eighty-fifth year.'

It is interesting in passing to note that a handful of men,
acting on some kind of premonition, did not sign on to
Titanic's crew, despite the scarcity of work at the time. In
her recollections for Southampton City Heritage Oral
History, a Mrs Burrows of Southampton stated: 'My son
Harry goes to sea, and he had stayed home for a month in
the expectation of getting engaged on the *Titanic*. He went
down to sign on, but at the last moment changed his mind
and came away, for which we are very thankful. I can't
explain why he changed his mind; some sort of feeling
came over him, he told me.' However, others, such as
Frederick Simmons, a twenty-five-year-old steward, had no
such sense of foreboding, as his letter posted from
Queenstown to his wife in Southampton indicates.

Just a line in great haste to let you know I am feeling fine,
and am rather pleased with the ship of course I don't know
if I shall have a show or not but I hope to. How are you
going on I hope you and baby are keeping very well. I
expect I shall be comfortable here, when you write please

address F. C. S. Simmons as there are 2 more of my name in the ship well darling I have no more to say now as I am in a hurry, love to all at home and heaps of it and kisses for you and teddy.
From your ever-loving husband
Fred
xxxxx
xxxxx
xxxxx
XXX

It should perhaps be mentioned that (much to White Star's distaste) seafarers were unionized by 1912. Indeed, seamen on *Olympic* soon after the wreck of *Titanic* went on strike because insufficient extra safety measures had been implemented. At first the managers tried to stick a charge of mutiny on them, but this was sensibly dropped. At the London inquiry following the wreck, the interests of the National Sailors' Union and the Firemen's [stokers'] Union were represented by Thomas Scanlan.

Liners as large as *Titanic* offered a wide variety of jobs. There were masters at arms and quartermasters, boatswains, nightwatchmen, trimmers, greasers, electricians, carpenters and even a window-cleaner. There were boiler-makers, lookouts, seamen and able seamen, all involved in running the ship. Looking after the passengers were the bakers, patissiers, specialized chefs, butchers, fishmongers, coffee-men, scullery hands, dishwashers, sommeliers, stewards and stewardesses, the gymnasium, swimming pool and Turkish bath staff, bootblacks, laundry staff, waiters, barmen, bed-makers and cleaners, a printer, the post-office clerks, the radio men, and the musicians, who travelled in second class on E deck, with a separate room for their instruments. As Violet Jessop (see pages 236–8) recalled: 'Even Jenny, the ship's cat and a member of the crew, immediately found herself a comfortable corner; she varied her usual Christmas routine on previous ships by presenting *Titanic* with a litter of kittens in April.' Sadly, Jenny and her kittens went down with *Titanic*, along with all the other pets on board.

In all, 913 crew looked after the ship and her 1,316 passengers, though as the *Liverpool Echo* reported on 11 April 1912, this was not full capacity: 'A full complement was not expected in Easter Week, more especially as the *Olympic* sailed last Wednesday (3 April) with a big list of passengers.' Drinking alcohol was, by the way, frowned on among crew members and, indeed, had been officially forbidden on White Star ships since the time of Thomas Ismay. Earnings varied greatly. Captain Smith, aged sixty-two and at the top of his profession, earned £105 a month. By contrast, the captain of the much smaller *Carpathia*, Arthur Rostron, who was forty-two at the time of the wreck, earned £53. A typical seaman's wage would be £5, and a lookout's 5 guineas. Assistant Radio Operator Harold Bride was well paid at £48 a month. A steward might earn £3 15s a month, and a stewardess £3 10s, but they could supplement their wages to an impressive extent through tips (especially in first class), and some had cordial relationships with passengers, which had developed over several voyages. It wasn't unusual for a passenger to seek out a particular steward, stewardess or waiter, and significantly, stewards and stewardesses were the only crew members routinely mentioned by name in passengers' letters and telegrams home.

Marconigrams cost 12s 6d (62½ pence) for the first ten words and 9d (4p) a word thereafter. Passengers sent and received over 250 of them between 10 and 14 April, so there was plenty of money sloshing about on board. An instance of this can be gathered by noting some of the items that went down with the ship:

- 3,364 bags of mail and about 750 parcels and packets
- 1 Renault motor car
- 1 marmalade machine
- 1 painting by Merry Joseph Blondel (a rather dreary mid-Victorian mannerist)
- 5 grand pianos
- 30 cases of golf clubs and tennis rackets
- 1 jewel-encrusted copy of *The Rubáiyát of Omar Khayyám*, supposedly the most expensive volume ever bound, which was on its way to an American who'd successfully bid for it at auction, parting with £405
- 4 cases of opium

According to Bruce Beveridge in *Titanic: The Ship Magnificent*, a Mrs James Cardeza occupied the palatial starboard-side parlour suite on *Titanic*. She was accompanied by her maid, her son and his manservant, together with 'fourteen trunks, four bags, a jewel-case and three packing-cases'. In a special case that she deposited for safe-keeping with the purser's office, she had jewellery worth $104,743 (the equivalent of about £1.6 million today). Among it was a pink diamond of 6⁷⁄₁₆ carats from Tiffany & Co., New York, for which she made an insurance claim against White Star of $20,000 (about £300,000 today).

As *Titanic* went down, more than one steward self-lessly ushered one or other of his charges into a lifeboat. Perhaps the happy atmosphere that had prevailed on board before the disaster made this sacrifice somewhat easier. Former assistant storekeeper Frank Prentice recalled in an interview given to *TV Times* in 1982, 'It was one merry party – the best of food, the best of dinner, orchestras, dancing – oh, they had a fine time.' A first-class passenger confirmed this in a glowing report to the *Belfast Evening Telegraph* on 15 April 1912 after disembarking at Queenstown:

'. . . but up where we were – some 60 feet above the waterline – there was no indication of the strength of the tossing swell below. This indeed is the one great impression I received from my first [*sic*] trip on the *Titanic* – and everyone with whom I spoke shared it – her wonderful steadiness. Were it not for the brisk breeze blowing along the decks, one would scarcely have imagined that every hour found us some 20 knots farther upon our course . . .

The lordly contempt of the *Titanic* for anything less

than a hurricane seemed most marvellous and comforting. But other things besides her steadiness filled us with wonder. Deck over deck and apartment after apartment lent their deceitful aid to persuade us that instead of being on the sea we were still on terra firma . . . After dinner as we sat in the beautiful lounge listening to the White Star orchestra playing the 'Tales of Hoffmann' and 'Cavalleria Rusticana' selection, more than once we heard the remark: 'You would never imagine we were on board a ship.' Still harder was it to believe that up on the top deck it was blowing a gale . . .

Lifts and lounges and libraries are not generally associated in the public mind with second class, yet in the *Titanic* all are found. It needed the assurance of our guide that we had left the saloon and were really in the second class.

On the crowded third-class deck were hundreds of English, Dutch, Italians and French mingling in happy fellowship, and when we wandered down among them we found that for them, too, the *Titanic* was a wonder. No more general cabins, but hundreds of comfortable rooms with two, four or six berths each, beautifully covered in red-and-white coverlets. Here, too, are lounges and smoking rooms, less magnificent than those amidships, to be sure, but nonetheless comfortable, and which, with the swivel chairs and separate tables in the dining rooms, struck me as not quite fitting in with my previous notion of steerage accommodation . . .

And then this morning, when the full Atlantic swell

came upon our port side, so stately and measured was the roll of the mighty ship that one needed to compare the moving of the side with the steady line of the clear horizon.

Not all passengers liked the Olympic-class liners' style, however. The journalist Edith Louise Rosenbaum, who travelled first class on *Titanic* (and survived), wrote to her secretary, 'I feel as if I were in a big hotel instead of on a cosy ship. Everyone is so stiff and formal. There are hundreds of help, bell-boys, stewards and stewardesses . . .'

SOUTHAMPTON

Number 44 Berth at Southampton, the new White Star deepwater dock, had been opened successfully on 14 June 1911 with *Olympic*'s maiden voyage to New York. Now it was *Titanic*'s turn. From the morning of 4 April (Maundy Thursday) until her departure, though, she was the focus of continuous work – right through the Easter holidays – as Andrews, Smith and their teams strove to get her ready for the passengers who would be boarding throughout the morning of 10 April. There were 4,427 extra tons of coal to be shipped, and the crew to be interviewed and signed on. Food and drink had to be loaded and stowed (in great quantities), as did the general cargo, the mails (at the last minute) and so forth.

Andrews can barely have slept, what with supervising the finessing of the liner, showing groups of bigwigs around, and having meetings with agents, subcontractors, fitters, officers and managers. Uniforms were commissioned from Millers, flowers from Bealing's, coal from Rea's and beer from Hibberts – and Andrews was everywhere in his untidy suit, enthusiastic, tireless and usually good-tempered. His Southampton secretary would note later: 'Through the various days that the vessel lay at Southampton, Mr Andrews was never idle. He generally left his hotel about 8.30 a.m. for the offices, where he dealt with his correspondence, then went on board until 6.30 p.m. . . . He would himself put in their place such things as racks, tables, chairs, berth ladders, electric fans, saying that except he saw everything right he would not be satisfied.'

And in the usual way of these things, miraculously, by the evening of Tuesday, 9 April, all was settled – pretty much! Andrews wrote to his wife Helen that night: 'The Titanic is now complete and will I think do the old firm credit tomorrow when we sail.'

From 9.30 a.m. on the following day many second- and third-class passengers began to arrive and board. From 11.30 a.m. the first-class passengers began to arrive, all brought down by special LSWR trains from London. Among them was William (W. T.) Stead, the sixty-two-year-old pioneering journalist and social reformer who campaigned against child prostitution, and who was travelling first class at the invitation of US President William Taft to take part in a peace conference to be held at Carnegie Hall. But Stead went down with the ship, having bravely helped women and children to lifeboats, and was reputedly last seen calmly reading a book in the first-class smoking room. It's interesting to note that Stead wrote a story, 'From the Old World to the New', in 1892, in which the RMS *Majestic* (White Star) rescues survivors of a ship that has crashed into an iceberg. (I mention this because of the notorious relevance of Morgan Robertson's apparently prescient novella of 1898 – 'Futility or The Wreck of the Titan'.) Stead left a widow and five children at home.

Another interesting passenger was the Jesuit priest Francis Browne, who travelled from Southampton to Queenstown. He was a keen amateur photographer, who took photos to a professional standard, and it is to him that we owe some of the pictorial record of *Olympic* and *Titanic*. A former classmate of the writer James Joyce, he was thirty-two at the time of his trip, and took first-class stateroom A37 across the deck from Thomas Andrews. Over the first two days at sea he made the acquaintance of a rich American couple who offered to stand him his fare to New York in exchange for his company. However, when Browne telegraphed his superior for permission, he got an unambiguous reply: 'GET OFF THAT SHIP.' He spent the First World War as an Irish Guards chaplain, and in later life his ministry took him all over the world. He died in Dublin in 1960, and his library of more than 42,000 photographs lay forgotten until it was rediscovered in 1986 by a fellow priest who was aware of the photographs' worth.

Finally, no short passenger list for *Titanic* would be complete without mentioning Michel Navratil, who sailed on the liner with his two young sons, aged three and four. The boys were put into Collapsible D, the last lifeboat successfully launched from the stricken ship, but Navratil himself went down with *Titanic*. His body was recovered by CS *Mackay-Bennett*, and among his effects was a loaded revolver.

'Michel Navratil, who was born in Slovakia, died on *Titanic* in his thirty-second year. He had married the Italian Marcelle Caretto in 1907 and had two sons by her: Michel junior, born in 1908, and Roger, born in 1910. The family had settled in Nice.

When the couple separated at the beginning of 1912, the boys were placed in the custody of their mother, though Michel senior was granted visiting rights. The boys were with him at Easter, 1912, but he abducted them, fleeing France for England via Monte Carlo. Navratil booked three second-class tickets on *Titanic* while staying at the Charing Cross Hotel with his sons, and took ship with them under the name of Louis Hoffmann. He told the other passengers that he was a widower, taking his sons to a new life in the States. On the night of the wreck, Michel junior remembered, 'My father entered our cabin where we were sleeping. He dressed me very warmly and took me in his arms. A stranger did the same for my brother. When I think of it now, I am very moved. They knew they were going to die.'

EMBARKATION

Third-class passengers were the first to board, on account of their large numbers, and their need to be carefully directed to their quarters. They were treated attentively and courteously. First- and second-class passengers embarked a few hours later – up to within an hour of departure – and, as much because of the sheer height of *Titanic* as class distinctions, entry was by separate companionways on different levels. Second-class passengers boarded at C deck promenade. First-class passengers arrived later, and were greeted on arrival by the captain, while stewards fussed over their usually copious luggage.

'It is in more ways than one a very ugly business, and a mere scrape along the ship's side, so slight that, if reports are to be believed, it did not interrupt a card party in the gorgeously fitted (but in chaste style) smoking room – or was it in the delightful French café? – is enough to bring on the exposure. All the people on board existed under a sense of false security. How false, it has been sufficiently demonstrated. And the fact which seems undoubted, that some of them were actually reluctant to enter the boats when told to do so, shows the strength of that falsehood. Incidentally it shows also the sort of discipline on board these ships, the sort of hold kept on the passengers in the face of the unforgiving sea. These people seemed to imagine it an optional matter, whereas the order to leave the ship should be an order of the sternest character, to be obeyed unquestioningly and promptly by everyone on board, with men to enforce it at once, and to carry it out methodically and swiftly. And it is no use to say it cannot be done, for it can. It has been done. The only requisite is manageableness of the ship herself and of the numbers she carries on board. That is the great thing which makes for safety. A commander should be able to hold his ship and everything on board of her in the hollow of his hand, as it were. But with the modern foolish trust in material, and with those floating hotels, this has become impossible. A man may do his best, but he cannot succeed in a task which from greed, or more likely from sheer stupidity, has been made too great for anybody's strength.'

Joseph Conrad, 'Some Reflections on the
Loss of the *Titanic*' (1912), collected
in *Notes on Life and Letters*, 1921

THE VOYAGE BEGINS

At last, following an hour's delay after a near-collision with the much-smaller liner SS *City of New York* in Southampton harbour, *Titanic* set sail for Cherbourg (70 miles away) at 1.00 p.m. on Wednesday, 10 April. She arrived in Cherbourg at 6.30 p.m., where the tenders *Traffic* and *Nomadic* disembarked 22 passengers and boarded 274 (*Titanic* was too large for the harbour, so had to stand off). The liner departed from Cherbourg at 8.10 p.m. and arrived at Queenstown (now called Cobh) at 11.30 a.m. on the following day. Here 7 passengers disembarked, 113 more came aboard, and another 1,385 sacks of mail were loaded.

Titanic's stay here was short. At 1.30 p.m. she set sail again to meet her fatal destiny only eighty-four hours later. The disaster was followed by two inquiries, at which Harland & Wolff and White Star played it all down as far as they could. There was, of course, a mass of publicity, popular songs and even toys. The German company Steiff, famous for its teddy bears, produced a black-furred 'mourning' bear complete with black eyes, red-rimmed from crying. These 'Titanic' bears are very rare nowadays, and at auction one in good condition might fetch £100,000.

'Millionaire Benjamin Guggenheim's mistress, the Parisian singer Leontine Aubart, known as Ninette, who survived the wreck, wrote to White Star from New York on 1 May 1912, itemizing the property she'd lost. She was very methodical, and her list gives a good idea of the copious luggage richer Edwardian women travelled with:

Trunks
• 1 trunk 'Innovation' for hats
• 1 trunk 'Innovation' for dresses

- 1 trunk 'Innovation' for lingerie
- 1 trunk 'Vuitton'
- 1 toilet-bag with silver fittings ... 3,500 French Francs (FF)
- 24 dresses and wraps ... 25,000 FF
- 7 hats and 2 with aigrettes [egret plumage] ... 2,400 FF

Shoes
- 6 pairs black
- 6 pairs evening
- 6 pairs satin with jewelled buckles
- 6 other pairs ... 1,800 FF

Lingerie
- 24 chemises
- 6 chemisettes
- 12 sets of knickers
- 24 night costumes of silk lace, corsets, corset-covers
- Handkerchiefs and neck-wear ... 6,000 FF
- Gloves and opera glasses ... 400 FF

Jewellery
- 1 gold bag with sapphires ... 4,000 FF
- 1 purse, gold with emeralds ... 2,000 FF
- 1 money and powder purse, gold with sapphires ... 4,000 FF
- 1 bracelet ... 3,000 FF
- 1 tiara of brilliants ... 9,000 FF

Total: 61,100 FF (about £35,000 today)

Mlle Aubart filed a formal claim for damages later, and affixed a copy of this list and the letter it comprised to it. This document was witnessed, signed and sealed by Hanson C. Coxe, the US Deputy Consul-General in Paris on 20 February 1913. Mlle Aubart also put in a claim for personal injury; her total claim amounted to $37,220 (about £550,000 today). Her petition was finally filed by her US attorney, A. Gordon Murry, on 10 April 1913 – a year to the day from the date of *Titanic*'s departure from Southampton.'

CHAPTER TWELVE

REBUILDING

FOUR PEOPLE ON A RAINY day in southern England. They are all skilled engineers and have come together at the British Engineerium in Hove to take up the challenge of rebuilding several elements of *Titanic*.

The Engineerium itself, built in the late Victorian era, was originally the pumping station that supplied water to Brighton and Hove. Restoration on it began in 1976, when it was reborn partly as a museum of engineering, and partly as a centre where skilled mechanics and engineers could restore machinery of the period for other industrial museums around the country. Latterly, the trust that ran it sold it to a private developer, and it is closed for refurbishment, so it is the ideal place for the team of four enthusiasts to go through their paces in their efforts to reconstruct some of the machinery and mechanical facilities that were carried on board the great liner, though this won't be their only location – they are working country-wide, wherever heavy engineering facilities still exist, from

Belfast, *Titanic*'s birthplace, to Sheffield – to tackle a whole range of challenges connected with the building of a great liner.

The Engineerium's rooms contain the original boilers for driving the pump engines – massive black beasts carbuncled with huge rivets, and reminiscent of *Titanic*'s own boilers, though far smaller – and a miniature railway track that once carried small trucks of coal to feed them.

In the adjoining hall sits the survivor of an original pair of beam engines that did the pumping. This has been lovingly preserved, its steel and brass parts gleaming under a sheen of oil and grease, and its huge flywheel which drove the giant pumping arm – both dwarfing any mere human – dominating the hall in which it stands.

The four people involved in the *Titanic* project – Yewande, Luke, Brendan and Dave – under the watchful eye of their 'foreman', Hadrian Spooner, and his assistant, Jim Milner, are having a hard time. They are attempting to bend a long, L-bend girder, red-hot from a furnace, into shape on a metal peg-board, the pegs hammered in along a predetermined curve to hold the girder steady as it's beaten into shape. The plan is to finish a 30-foot section of *Titanic*'s stem, or bow, to be erected in Belfast as a permanent memorial to the workers who built the liner.

The rain doesn't help. 'It was like hammering a boiling, slippery snake,' Dave said later. Yewande remembered her hair being singed even when she was standing a yard away. They'd been handling a 9-foot length of steel, 13 inches thick and weighing about 3 tons, which had been heated for thirty-six hours to a temperature of 2,000 degrees Celsius. Originally, the workers would have had little protective clothing. The team are using original materials and methods, but because of the sheer danger of the tasks in hand, they'll be adhering to modern health and safety standards throughout. Similarly, where authentic machine tools no longer exist, more recent or modern ones will be brought into play.

They don't get it right the first time, or the second, and tempers unravel a bit, but they stick to it, guided by Hadrian, and at last the job is done.

Drilling rivet holes into the successfully curved girder, then actually riveting all the component parts together, will come later. Brendan remembers standing in the well of the great Thompson Graving Dock in Belfast, now no longer in use and under threat of being filled in since its elderly gates would have to be replaced if they were to continue to keep out the waters of the Langan. The cost of that, for what is a huge museum piece, could be prohibitive. He found standing in the dock an awesome experience, but moving too, for in the debris on the floor he noticed a few ancient, rusting rivets, and wondered if some of them might have been intended for use on the Olympic-class liners of 1909–13.

THE PARTICIPANTS

Drawn to this project by curiosity about engineering history, a desire to learn more of the industrial techniques of the past, enthusiasm and a spirit of adventure, the four participants were selected after a series of rigorous auditions by the Twenty Twenty Television production team from a huge number of applicants.

Yewande Akinola

A Nigerian national who has lived in Britain since 2003, Yewande Akinola works for the international engineering firm Arup, who have been totally supportive of her involvement in the *Titanic* project, and were happy to let her have a short 'sabbatical' to pursue it.

Her degree was in engineering design, a branch of mechanical engineering, and appropriate technologies – low-energy, low-maintenance and low-intensive manufacture for the developing world. She has hands-on experience of many on-site construction methods, including welding, which she put to good use on the *Titanic* project.

As a child she used to make models of dream homes, which is what initially drew her to engineering, and what particularly attracted her to the *Titanic* project: she's interested in the idea of a 'building' as palatial as *Titanic*, but she also wanted to learn more about the people who worked and travelled on the liners of those days – 'How did they fit into those tiny beds?' She was also keen to find out more about the role women played in industry at the beginning of the last century.

Asked if all four of the team members get on, she grins and replies, 'Well, we've had our moments.' But it is clear that basically the team have really gelled – a very important thing when the key to the success of such a project is teamwork.

Luke Perry

Luke comes from a line of Black Country chain-makers that reaches back four generations. In fact, the family engineering business, currently celebrating its centenary, is one of the last UK factories that still makes bespoke chain (or cable) the same size as that used on *Titanic*.

Born in the Black Country, Luke still works and lives in the area. His work as a trained sculptor has increasingly led him to explore industrial history and to commemorate Britain's industrial past. The Black Country, which he sees as integral to world history, remains a fascinating place for him, and he has set up a non-profit company called Industrial Heritage Stronghold to champion the region. Luke is no stranger to monumental, industrially inspired sculpture, and his company has been responsible for a number of important pieces around the country. His *Monument to the Fall of Black Country Industry*, also known as the *Cradley Column*, stands in Cradley Heath, while his *Steel Manifesto* is a tribute to basic qualities such as honesty and free will. It's a 2-ton, 15-foot-long series of slabs of steel laid end to end and bears the following words:

Give us the truth and let us make our own decisions.
Do not feed us bullshit to pre-empt a reaction that you
    don't know we'll have.
You must trust in people's better natures to make choices
    that are theirs to make.
Liberty is not relative.

> We must allow our equalities to unite us before our
>   differences tear us apart.
> The responsibility belongs to all.

He was drawn to the *Titanic* project because of his fascination with the engineering techniques of a century ago, though he acknowledges that the working conditions of those days were appalling: 'No one would have wanted their kids to work in such circumstances, but on the other hand, they had great pride in what they did.'

Brendan Walker

Brendan describes himself as a thrill engineer. As a child, he loved making fireworks. His background is in engineering, and he worked at British Aerospace for the first five years of his career, whilst studying aeronautical engineering at Imperial College, London. But after that he made a career change, retraining and taking an MA in industrial design engineering at the Royal College of Art (RCA).

The author of *The Taxonomy of Thrill*, Brendan has worked with teams designing rides and events for such places as Alton Towers and Thorpe Park, where a key aim is to balance the maximum amount of thrill – often created from an increase in perceived risk – with the real risks and dangers of causing harm to life or limb. 'The most important thing to remember when creating a roller-coaster is the choreography. It's not just about loops and drops, but about theatre, tempo and understanding your audience.'

Fascinated by the psychology of thrill, he describes himself as the world's only thrill engineer, and his work fuses engineering and psychological skills with those of a true artist.

As far as the *Titanic* project is concerned, he was most attracted by the prospect of hands-on, computer-free engineering work. Brendan had lots of hands-on experience when he was training and is fascinated by the heavy-engineering aspect of reconstructing elements of the great liner. In addition, he loves thinking on his feet and problem-solving. He says that the team would look at a huge part of the structure and think, 'What tool would they have used for that?' and 'How could this possibly have worked?' Slightly on the lighter side, one of Brendan's personal *Titanic* projects was to carve the head of the electrical exercise horse in oak. It was, he says, 'a bit like crafting a very large sex toy'! Which it could well be, though on reflection, it's more reminiscent in its basic form of the Loch Ness Monster's head!

Dave Wilkes

Born and bred in Hackney, east London, Dave now lives in Cambridgeshire. He is a steelworker well used to spending his days 300 feet up in the air working on the steel frameworks of high-rise buildings. Inevitably, he's had his moments of danger, like when he fell off a building. Fortunately, his clothing caught on a girder, which saved his life. He'd have been killed if he'd hit the ground a good 70 feet below.

An all-rounder, Dave has an encyclopaedic knowledge of a wide range of tools and trades. In his time he's worked as a roofer and plumber, but he has an especially keen knowledge of metalwork and its associated machinery. Metalwork even takes up his spare time – his hobbies include making wrought-iron gates and candelabra – but he's been working with iron and steel since he left school at the age of sixteen.

Despite his fall, working at great heights doesn't bother him at all – his grandfather was a steeplejack, which has made him interested in how often a trade can run in a family. His interest in *Titanic* stems from a love of art nouveau and early art deco design, so the liner's interiors had a special draw for him, but the box-girder, building-like steel framework of the ship attracted his curiosity as well. His participation in the *Titanic* project allows him to pay tribute to those of his grandparents' generation and earlier who worked so hard to make British industry the envy of the world, once upon a time. Among the fun parts of the project, he remembers, was going to Nice to spend time on a luxury, high-tech modern yacht, which cost £53 million to build and charters at €350,000 per week, to experience one of the world's most electrically advanced ships – an accolade given to *Titanic* in her own day.

RECONSTRUCTION BEGINS

The team faced a diverse range of tasks. They had to reconstruct a large section of *Titanic*'s stem, find out all about the dangerous and skilled craft of hand-riveting, and oversee the casting of a replica of one of her anchors, weighing 16.1 tons (this last was done in Sheffield, since the heavy plant that existed in Dudley in *Titanic*'s day no longer exists). It was delivered to its final resting place in Netherton – the town where Noah Hingley's company cast the original anchors – on a dray pulled by twenty shire horses, recreating a moment in history. They also had to reconstruct one of *Titanic*'s dynamos and a Marconi radio, from which they attempted to transmit a transatlantic message from Cornwall to Newfoundland, as had been done in 1901. In addition they recreated other internal elements of *Titanic*, including the kind of crockery on which dinner would have been served, some stained glass, panelling and furniture as used in the first-class smoking room, and some furnishings and equipment of a third-class cabin. Using a replica oven they had reproduced (though it is welded together rather than cast), they also had to cook a meal from one of Titanic's menus. Another project they faced was to reconstruct one of the electric exercise horses from the gymnasium.

Titanic, we should remember, was as much a fun palace as a working ship, and both functions were responsible for the innovations in her design. But we should also bear in mind that it is quite possible, given the German sabre-rattling that was going on well in advance of Britain's declaration of war against the Kaiser in early August 1914, that the Olympic-class liners were designed with the idea of one day converting them into troop or hospital ships.

The tasks the team were going to undertake were

divided into five programmes for the TV series. Episode one focused on the reconstruction of the stem while also exploring the industrial might of the early twentieth century. The second episode, featuring the reconstruction of the first-class smoking room and the third-class cabin, also examined the class divisions that permeated British society in those days, and took a look at the Edwardian arts and crafts movement and the interior designers who worked the ship. Episode three dealt with the first leg of *Titanic*'s voyage, from Belfast to Southampton, examined the casting of the mighty anchor, and looked at the miners' strike of 1912, which almost prevented the liner sailing at all. Electricity was the theme of the fourth episode, which covered the innovations ushered in by this new form of power. It also dealt with how much passenger facilities were improved for those travelling on the Olympic-class ships, showed how meals were prepared and served, and looked at what was on the menus. The final episode explored the strengths and weaknesses of the health and safety measures – both those that prevailed during construction and those on the completed ship – and concluded with an overview of the fatal wreck.

On a typical day at the Engineerium the team worked separately and together on several projects in tandem. One such day, when Dave was filming elsewhere with the Social History Unit, ran as follows.

Outside the main workshop of the Engineerium is a yard, where a modern electric furnace, which looks rather like an industrial barbecue, has been set up. Hadrian pours wet coke on to hot embers to top the thing up, and it hisses and spits. 'Stand clear,' he advises. 'These things can crack and shoot fragments out.' The rest of us obey.

The oven, a massive shining steel artefact, which will be brought in later for the doors and elements to be fitted, stands near by. Luke's job today is working on the oven doors, which he's already manufactured. They're made of steel, with iron brackets and brass trimming, which he'll buff later with a machine driven by compressed air. Yewande will help him by following through with Brasso, a product marketed in Britain by Reckitt & Sons since 1905. Nowadays this mild solvent and extremely fine abrasive is also used to polish CDs, DVDs and screens in order to repair scratches.

Luke has used a lathe to turn the brass handles of the oven doors, and these need to be bent to an angle of some 45 degrees before fitting. Bending brass under heat is a delicate job, and something Luke hasn't undertaken before. Under Hadrian's watchful eye, he clamps a handle in a vice and heats it until the metal at the joint is a dull, dark red. Then he stretches and turns the metal, to prevent it cracking or breaking. The job is a success and Luke is extremely pleased.

Luke is making the oven doors more or less on his own, but in Harland & Wolff's workshops there would probably have been a production line. Even so, he makes the point that the first oven door takes the longest time. The more you get used to what's needed and how to put the component parts together, the shorter the time it takes to complete each one. Thus, while the first may have taken him four hours, the second will take three, the third probably two, and the last as little as one hour.

The oven itself – essentially Luke's baby, though Yewande helps him on it – cannot exactly replicate the original. In the original, all the electric heating elements would have been live and uninsulated, so touching one would have meant certain death. The only safety device was that the elements wouldn't ignite if the doors weren't shut. In the reproduction, a fuse-box has to be installed on the side, and the elements must be properly covered.

In the early days of electricity there was no thermostatic control on the oven – it was either on or off. It had two elements, one on each side, and the degree of heat produced by each was indicated by thermometers outside the oven. By reading these, the cooks could regulate the heat by switching one or other element on or off, and presumably take into account the cooking that continued during the cooling-down period. It would be very interesting to know what the gastronomic standards were in comparison with those of a high-end modern restaurant. But that will be revealed when the team uses the oven to cook a full meal of several courses . . .

In the course of the day, Luke comes a cropper twice. He bores all the drill holes in an oven door when he should have left one undrilled for filming purposes. Depending on the schedule, he might have to solder one hole up again in order to re-drill it for TV. Later on, he realizes that he's drilled the holes using too wide a drill-bit anyway. He gets a good-natured ticking-off from Hadrian, but it's worth remembering that Harland & Wolff's rules for their workers – and there's a copy of them posted on the wall of the workshop here – are ferocious. Had Luke been a worker on *Titanic*, he'd have had his wages docked at the very least.

Meanwhile, Brendan, with Yewande, has been making freehand technical drawings – his apparent effortlessness is totally enviable – for the design of the reconstructed electrical exercise horse. This must be very basic stuff for them. One of the component parts is an off-centred steel spindle that is integral to simulating the jogging motion of a real animal. But the prepared part is too big, and Brendan has to spend a very patient day on the lathe paring it down by 80 per cent – a job that takes five hours, not counting setting and resetting the lathe to cut down, first, the larger cylinder of the spindle and, second, the smaller, off-centred lug. The lathe itself, constructed in the 1950s and still in production, is a 'Keighley' model, worth at least £11,000 today. 'The Rolls-Royce of lathes', Hadrian calls it. But it's a long and nit-picking day for Brendan because the job requires one's full attention while at the same time being seriously dull. It's not something a man with his kind of mind would easily take to, though it's part and parcel of the process of manufacturing. And if it takes so long on a more or less modern lathe, imagine how long the work would have taken on an Edwardian model.

Yewande is working with Jim Milner on another part of the 'horse'. One of the components calls for a strip of heavy steel to be heated and shaped into a U-form. The steel strip, some 6 feet long, is placed in the open-air furnace and heated for about half an hour. Then Yewande, wearing heavy gloves, must take the ends (only the central part has been in the furnace) and quickly bend it around a low cylindrical form fixed to the edge of the furnace. This isn't easy as the metal is heavy and stubborn, and cools fast once out of the furnace, but she does it. Later she'll cut and fix a bar to the centre of the U's curve, using an oxyacetylene torch.

Lunch is a barbecue eaten in the open air and, in accordance with typical British early summer rules, after what has been a perfect morning, the clouds gather over and the drizzle that follows soon gives way to pounding rain. Inside, TV director Ruari Fallon mentions that later in the week they'll be shooting on board a steam-driven Thames tug before returning to Hove to work on the reconstruction of the first-class smoking room. For the latter they'll be making a tub chair of the type installed on *Titanic*, a table and some of the panelling, all under the supervision of an expert carpenter. They'll also be recreating some of *Titanic*'s stained glass, and reconstructing a third-class cabin. When completed, all these items will be donated to the Ulster Folk and Transport Museum in Belfast.

In the afternoon, work resumes under cover. The days can be long, sometimes starting at 7.00 a.m. and continuing until 9.00 p.m., but the challenge always remains stimulating. Someone expresses regret that, unlike the *Queen Elizabeth*, the *Queen Mary* and the *QE2*, the RMS

Olympic, first and sole survivor of her class, was broken up rather than kept on as a museum, or a floating hotel or casino. At least then we would have retained an authentic remnant of those glory days of transatlantic travel. Alas, business thinking didn't work like that in the first half of the twentieth century. What survived did so by chance, so only a fraction of our industrial and maritime heritage remains to be seen. These TV programmes, though, attempt to rectify that situation, and pay due respect to the engineers and workers of the not-so-distant past.

REFERENCES

Bibliography

Many books have been written about *Titanic*, most of them focusing on the wreck, but that is not the purpose of this particular volume. The list that follows is short, but it does include Bruce Beveridge's brilliant, exhaustive, expensive and massive two-volume work, which may be considered the standard modern work.

Bruce Beveridge (with Scott Andrews, Steve Hall and Daniel Klistorner), *Titanic: The Ship Magnificent*, 2 vols – *Design and Construction* and *Interior Design and Fitting Out* (The History Press, Stroud, 2009)

James Brown, *Signalling* (James Brown & Son, Glasgow, 1908), now published as *Brown's Signalling: How to Learn the International Code of Visual and Sound Signals*

Shan F. Bullock, *Thomas Andrews, Shipbuilder* (Maunsel & Co., Dublin and London, 1912)

Joseph Conrad, 'Some Reflections on the Loss of the Titanic'

(1912), collected in *Notes on Life and Letters* (Dent, London, 1921)

Duncan Crosbie, *Le Titanic*, trans. Frédérique Fraisse (Quatre Fleuves, Paris, 2007)

Michael Davie, *The Titanic: The Full Story of a Tragedy* (Bodley Head, London,1986)

Robin Gardiner, *Titanic: The Ship That Never Sank?* (Ian Allen, Hersham, 2009)

Tony Gibbons, *A Technical Directory of Battleships and Battlecruisers, 1860–present* (Salamander, London, 1983)

Lady Duff Gordon, *Discretions and Indiscretions* (Frederick A. Stokes, London, 1932)

Stephen Gwynn, *The Famous Cities of Ireland* (Maunsel & Co., Dublin, 1915)

Archibald Campbell Holms, *Practical Shipbuilding* (1918)

Donald Hyslop, Alastair Forsyth, Sheila Jemima, *Titanic Voices: Memories from the Fateful Voyage* (Alan Sutton, Stroud, 1997)

Violet Jessop, *Titanic Survivor: The Memoirs of a Stewardess*, ed. John Maxtone-Graham (Alan Sutton, Stroud, 1998)

Walter Lord, *A Night to Remember* (Penguin, London, 1981)

John Maxtone-Graham, *The Only Way to Cross* (Macmillan, London, 1972)

Michael McCaughan, *The Birth of the Titanic* (Blackstaff, Belfast, 1998)

David Miller, *The Illustrated Directory of Warships, 1860–present* (London, Salamander, 2001)

Morgan Robertson, *Futility or The Wreck of the Titan* (Kessinger Reprints, Lavergne, Montana, 2009)

Robert Sherard, *The White Slaves of England* (James Bowden, London, 1897)

William Stead, 'From the Old World to the New' (1892)

Frederick Talbot, *Steamship Conquest of the World* (Heinemann, London, 1912)

Brendan Walker, *The Taxonomy of Thrill* (Aerial Publishing, 2004)

Webography

There are many sites concerned with *Titanic*. The best to start with are:

titanichistoricalsociety.org
encyclopedia-titanica.org
keyflux.com/titanic/facts.htm
titanic-titanic.com

Filmography

There are, of course, many films about *Titanic*. Those listed below are either the best or at least the best known. Several television and documentary films have been omitted, though it's worth mentioning Dr Robert Ballard's *Secrets of the Titanic* (1987). Feature films include the following:

A Night to Remember, **directed by Roy Ward Baker (1958)**
Although it has some factual errors – arising from matters related to the sinking that were not known when it was made – this is one of the best feature films.

Titanic, directed by Herbert Selpin (1943)

A German propaganda film, this was supposed to focus on British imperialism and incompetence. It flopped even in Germany, but clips were lifted for use in Roy Ward Baker's film *A Night to Remember*.

Titanic, directed by Jean Negulesco (1953)

Starring Barbara Stanwyck, Clifton Webb and Robert Wagner, this lavish documentary-drama mixed fictional and real characters. It opened in Hollywood on 14 April, exactly forty-one years after the disaster.

Raise the Titanic, directed by Jerry Jameson (1980)

Based on a Clive Cussler novel, this film boasted the likes of Alec Guinness and Jason Robards in its cast, but it was an expensive flop. Its producer, Lord Lew Grade, was prompted to exclaim, 'Raise the Titanic? My God, it would be cheaper to lower the Atlantic!'

Titanic, directed by James Cameron (1997)

Starring Leonardo di Caprio and Kate Winslet, this romantic melodrama won eleven Oscars, but told a love story that was highly unlikely given the social divisions of the time.

Titanic Societies

There are several societies worldwide, but the most well known are probably:

The Titanic Historical Society, Inc.
(www.titanichistoricalsociety.org)

The Titanic International Society
(www.titanicinternationalsociety.org)

GLOSSARY

Abaft – towards the stern of a ship.

Abeam – across the ship, from side to side.

Aft – towards the rear of a ship.

Amidships – area around the centre of a ship.

Anchor – a heavy metal weight used to moor a ship to the seabed. *Bower anchors* were the main anchors, so called because they were carried in the bows (at the front) of a ship. *Kedge anchors*, small and made of iron, were used for hauling a ship around if it went aground. *Stockless anchors* had no crosspiece at the top of the shaft, thus enabling them to be close-hauled into the anchor hawse (the hole into which the anchor fits when wound in).

Anneal – to soften metal by heating and then slowly cooling.

Astern – beyond the rear end of a ship; also used to describe the action of reversing a ship, e.g. 'go astern', 'full astern'.

Athwart – from side to side of a ship.

Ballast – any heavy weight, e.g. sand, pig-iron or water, carried low down in a ship to dress or balance her; it can be expelled or taken in as necessary.

Beam – the width of a ship at her widest point.

Berth – bed (often a bunk) aboard ship; also a cabin, or the position of a ship in dock.

Bilge – the almost flat part of a ship's bottom where propeller shafts' water tends to collect.

Binnacle – housing for the compass, made of brass to prevent interference from any iron near by.

Blue Peter – rectangular blue flag with white rectangle at its centre, the signal for imminent departure of a ship.

Boatswain (pronounced 'bosun') – petty officer in charge of deck crew, gear, lifeboats, rigging and so on.

Bossing – steel-plate casing used for propeller shafts.

Bow – forepart of a ship.

Bridge (also navigating bridge) – usually, and always on modern ships, enclosed area to the fore of a ship's superstructure from where she is steered.

Bulkhead – principally athwart-ship's dividing walls, but in fact any dividing wall aboard; watertight bulkheads are partitions of reinforced metal plating designed to withstand the influx of water in a wreck.

Bulwark – the protective rail around the deck of a ship.

Burgee – triangular or swallow-tailed flag.

Bushings – high-voltage conductor insulators.

Cable – usually refers to the heavy steel wire or chain-link that attaches an anchor to its capstan.

Capstan – horizontal turning-wheel by which, for example, an anchor is raised and lowered; it was steam-powered on *Titanic*.

Caulk – to make watertight by stuffing material in between any joined edges that are not flush.

Chain lockers – spaces or compartments in which anchor cable is stowed.

Chart room – map room adjoining the bridge of a ship.

Chronometer, marine – finely accurate timepiece used to measure longitude, and thus determine the position of a ship.

Clinker-built – a method of building ships or boats with overlapping planks, giving the hull a stepped appearance.

Clipper – a fast sailing ship, so named because it clipped or shortened the journey time usually taken by other fast ships.

Coaming – a raised edge of wood or steel surrounding the opening of a hatch, bulkhead or deckhouse, and designed to strengthen it.

Coir – tough fibre from the outer husk of coconuts, used for making ropes and matting.

Companionway – a staircase leading from a deck to cabins below; probably a corruption of the Dutch word *companje*, meaning 'cabin'.

Crow's nest – a lookout point at the top of the foremast.

CS – Cable Ship.

Cutter – a small vessel, ready for instant launch in an emergency, such as man overboard; could also act as an auxiliary lifeboat.

Davit – a crane used to raise and lower lifeboats.

Deckhouse – a steel or wooden structure that encloses an area on deck, such as the bridge or the wheelhouse.

Derrick – a type of crane used on board ships.

Double-bottom – the space between the inner and outer 'skins' of a ship.

Draft – depth of a ship below the waterline.

Elliptical counter-stern – deck and knuckle line roughly elliptical in shape.

Ensign – national flag of a country, designed to be flown at sea. Britain has three (white, red and blue), but some countries, e.g. the USA, fly the same ensign as the land flag, while others (e.g. France) have ensigns only very subtly different from the land flag.

Fairwater – a cone-shaped cap used to streamline a propeller joint.

Faying – the process of nipping joints together with special blunt-ended chisels.

Fireman – stoker on board ship; his job was to keep the furnace topped up with coal.

Forecastle (pronounced 'foc-sul') – the front part of a ship, traditionally where the crew's quarters are situated.

Fore/forward – towards the front of a ship.

Greaser – engine maintenance man.

Gudgeons – lugs forged or cast on the stern-post from which the rudder is hung.

Halyards – light lines for rigging flags and yards.

Hawse pipes – holes at the bows through which anchor cables are fed.

Hawser – a heavyweight wire cable or chain.

Heads – an archaic name for the bows of a ship, which also became the nautical word for 'lavatories' because these facilities were originally situated over the bows.

Helm – steering gear.

HMHS – His/Her Majesty's Hospital Ship.

HMS – His/Her Majesty's Ship.

HMSS – His/Her Majesty's Steam Ship.

HMT – His/Her Majesty's Transport.

In-and-out system – a method of laying steel plating, in which the plates are laid one over another alternately.

Keel – the massive 'backbone' of steel that runs along the bottom of a ship.

Keelson – the supports or strengthener of the keel.

Knot – a nautical mile: 1 knot equals about 6,080 feet or 1.151 miles. It is exactly one-sixtieth of a degree of longitude on the Equator.

Lay down – to start building a ship by the keel.

Oakum – fibre obtained by unpicking old rope, often used for caulking.

Orlop deck – usually a partial, overlapping deck, often at the lowest level; its name comes from the Dutch word *overlopen*, meaning 'to cover or extend'.

Painter – a length of rope attached to the bow of a small boat for mooring or towing.

Pig-iron – cheap iron cast in roughly rectangular ingots. The moulds used were part of a branching structure formed in sand, with many individual ingots at right angles to a central channel or runner. The configuration is similar to a litter of piglets suckling a sow – hence the name.

Pintle – a pin on the rudder corresponding to gudgeons.

Plate – steel or other metal rolled or sometimes cast in 'planks' for sheeting a ship's hull.

Poop deck – the aftermost and highest deck on a ship. The name, derived from the Latin *puppim*, meaning 'doll' or 'image', relates to the ancient practice of sailors keeping a representation of a deity on the highest deck to keep them safe.

Port – the nautical term for the left-hand side of a ship, looking forward.

POSH – Port Out Starboard Home, supposedly the best way to travel to India and the Far East to minimize exposure to the sun.

Quartermaster – petty officer in charge of the navigation instruments and steering the ship.

Reciprocating engine – piston engine, designed to convert steam into work.

RMS – Royal Mail Steamship.

Rudder – a flat piece of wood or steel, hinged vertically, and used for steering a boat or ship.

Sacrificial anodes – slabs or strips of zinc (or nowadays special alloys) placed over parts of a ship particularly vulnerable to corrosion.

Scantlings – the dimensions of a ship's frame, girders and plating.

Scarf – joint made by notching the ends of two pieces of timber or metal so that they lock together end to end.

Schooner – a sailing ship with two or more masts, using fore and aft sails (i.e. not square-rigged), and having a forward mast no taller than the others. The rig originated in Holland c.1600, but the etymology of the name is disputed: it is thought to come from the Scottish dialect word *scoon*, meaning 'skim'.

Scuppers – holes in the side of a ship that allow water to drain off the deck.

Scuttle – a hole with a lid used for coal-loading.

Shroud – a yard or rope that supports a mast.

Slip – a runway on which a ship was built to allow easy transition from land to sea.

SS – Steam Ship.

Starboard – the nautical term for the right-hand side of a ship, looking forward.

Stateroom – elegant word for a cabin.

Steerage – the cheapest and humblest accommodation for passengers, often in the lowest part of a ship, where the steering equipment was housed.

Stem – the prow or foremost part of a ship.

Stern – the aftermost part of a ship.

Strakes/straking – a continuous row of plates used in shipbuilding.

Telemotor – a hydraulic steering device.

Tonnage, gross registered – the overall tonnage officially registered for a ship.

Trimmer – an unskilled rating whose job was to keep firemen (stokers) supplied with coal.

TS – Turbine Ship.

Turbine – a rotary engine that extracts energy from a fluid, steam or airflow and converts it into useful work.

Warp – to haul a ship by rope to a fixed point.

Wheelhouse – the location of the ship's wheel, the place from where the ship is steered.

whp – water horsepower, a measure of energy applied to ship engines.

Windlass – horizontally mounted drum (also known as a capstan) for raising and lowering loads by means of a cable.

Wing-cabs – the compartments on either side of the navigation bridge from which a ship can be guided into port.

Yard – cylindrical spar slung across a mast and used to hang a sail from.

WEIGHTS AND MEASURES

In *Titanic*'s day, Great Britain still used the imperial system of weights and measures and these are what have been used in the text of this book. Exact metric equivalents are given below.

Length
1 inch = 25.4 mm
1 foot = 0.3048 m
1 yard = 0.9144 m
1 mile = 1.6093 km
1 knot = 1.852 km

Area
1 sq inch = 645.16 sq mm
1 sq foot = 929.0304 sq cm
1 sq yard = 0.8361 sq m
1 sq mile = 2.59 sq km (640 acres)

Liquid

1 pint = 20 fl oz = 0.5683 litres
1 quart = 1.1365 litres
1 gallon = 4.5461 litres

Weight

1 ounce = 28.3495 g
1 pound (lb) = 0.4536 kg
1 stone = 14 lb = 6.3503 kg
20 hundredweight (cwt) = 1 ton = 1.0160 tonnes

Speed

1 mile per hour = 1.6093 kph
1 knot per hour = 1.8518 kph

Heat

Freezing point of water: 32°F = 0°C
Boiling point of water: 212°F = 100°C

MONEY

In February 1971, after centuries of pounds, shillings and pence, Great Britain converted to a system of decimal currency. Here is an overview of how the two systems compare.

Farthing – one-quarter of an old penny, worth one-eighth of a new penny: this coin went out of circulation on 31 December 1960.

Halfpenny – one half of an old penny, worth one-quarter of a new penny: this coin went out of circulation on 31 July 1969.

Penny – expressed as 1d ('d' being short for 'denarius', the Latin word for a small silver Roman coin) and worth a bit less than one new halfpenny. (In fact, the new halfpenny was discontinued in December 1984 as having no practical worth any more.)

Threepenny bit – equivalent to 1¼ new pence.

Sixpenny bit – equivalent to 2½ new pence.

Shilling – expressed as 1s or 1/-; it was worth 12 pennies, equivalent to 5 new pence.

Florin – expressed as 2s or 2/-, equivalent to 10 new pence.

Half-crown – expressed as 2/6, equivalent to 12½ new pence.

Crown – worth 5 shillings (25p), this coin was not in general circulation because it was too large. It continues to be minted, but only for commemorative purposes.

Pound – £1 was worth 20 shillings or 240 old pennies. The latter weighed 1 lb, which gave the denomination its name. Originally a banknote, it was converted to a coin in 1983. (There was also a 10-shilling banknote until 1969; this was worth 50 new pence.)

Guinea – worth £1 1s, this gold coin was withdrawn from circulation in 1813 because its intrinsic value was greater than its face value. At livestock sales (and some art auctions) prices are quoted in guineas to this day.

Equivalents

It is very hard to put modern values on prices from *Titanic*'s day, partly because values are extremely relative. For example, a first-class crossing in a parlour suite would still seem prohibitively expensive, as would a dinner in the A La Carte Restaurant, whereas a double gin might seem incredibly cheap. As prices and purchasing power fluctuate with such volatility it is hard and possibly misleading to attempt relative values. However, this has been attempted in a few places in the text where it seems helpful to do so.

PICTURE CREDITS

Picture credits read clockwise from the top left-hand corner on each page/spread. NMNI = © National Museums Northern Ireland 2010/Collection Harland & Wolff
Photograph reproduced courtesy of the Trustees of National Museums Northern Ireland

First section

page 1: Harland & Wolff men leaving work, May 1911: NMNI/H1555

pages 2–3: J. P. Morgan (1837-1913): Topham Picturepoint/ TopFoto.co.uk; *Titanic* poster, 1912: courtesy of The Advertising Archives; Lord Pirrie and Bruce Ismay, 31 May 1911: NMNI/H23640; Thomas Andrews, 1911: NMNI/TR60-60A.

pages 4–5: Harland & Wolff drawing office, 1912: NMNI/H501; hydraulic riveters, *Britannic*, 1913: NMNI/H1919; turbine rotor being bladed, *Britannic*, 1914: NMNI/H1975.

pages 6–7: *Titanic*'s anchor leaving Hingley's works, 1 May 1911: © National Maritime Museum, Greenwich, London; *Olympic* funnel leaving workshops, 23 March 1911: NMNI/H2412; fitting the starboard tail shaft of *Titanic*, 1912: NMNI/H1557.

page 8: Port bow profile of *Olympic*: NMNI/H1515.

Second section

page 1: Stern view of completed *Titanic* being pulled by tugs, 1912, Belfast: NMNI/H1723.

pages 2–3: Artist's impression, second-class promenade deck, Titanic, 1912: Mary Evans Picture Library/Onslow Auctions Ltd; gymnasium, *Titanic*, 1912: Father Brown/Getty Images; first-class reading room, *Titanic*, 1912: Underwood & Underwood/ Corbis; first-class staircase on *Olympic*: Mary Evans Picture Library/Onslow Auctions Ltd.

pages 4–5: First-class suite, bedroom, *Titanic*, 1912: NMNI/H1725; artist's impression, second-class stateroom, *Titanic*, 1912: Mary Evans Picture Library/Onslow Auctions Ltd; third-class, two-berth stateroom, *Titanic*, 1912: NMNI; private bathroom, probably first class, *Titanic*: NMNI/H1530; artist's impression of one of the parlour suites on *Titanic*, 1912: Mary Evans Picture Library/Onslow Auctions Ltd.

pages 6–7: Capt. Smith and the officers of *Titanic*: NMNI/40253; John Jacob Astor, 1909: George Grantham Bain Collection, Library of Congress, Print and Photographs Division, Washington; passengers boarding *Titanic* from the tender *Ireland*, 10 April 1912: Father Browne/Getty Images; bridge, *Titanic*, 1912: The Granger Collection/TopFoto/TopFoto.co.uk.

page 8: *Titanic* leaving Queenstown, 11 April: Father Brown/ Getty Images; life-boats: Getty Images.

INDEX